# URBAN TOOLKIT

## WORKING WITH CITY ENVIRONMENTS

R. HOWLEY

E. OTTEN

gage EDUCATIONAL PUBLISHING COMPANY
A DIVISION OF CANADA PUBLISHING CORPORATION
TORONTO ONTARIO CANADA

**Copyright © 1991 Gage Educational Publishing Company**
A Division of Canada Publishing Corporation

**Canadian Cataloguing in Publication Data**

Howley, Robert, 1953–
  Urban toolkit

ISBN 0-7715-8169-6

1. City Planning – Problems, exercises, etc.

HT166.H69 1990     307.1'2076     C90-095168-0

**Gage Editorial Team**: Anne Marie Moro
                                    Carol Waldock

**Design**: Holly Fisher
**Cover illustration**: Chris Hayes
**Text illustration**: Josef Gardisch, Christine Partridge,
                                Anne Stanley

ISBN 0-7715-**8169-6**
1 2 3 4 5 FP 95 94 93 92 91
Written, Printed, and Bound in Canada

# Contents

# Introduction

Learning and discovery should be enjoyable, if not fun. When a person is actively involved in the learning process, then better learning takes place. The issues presented in this book are intended to encourage a renewed appreciation and understanding of the urban environment of which more and more of us find ourselves a part.

*Urban Toolkit* is an activity based book designed to explore the urban setting through dynamic mapping exercises, simulations, statistical analysis and innovative case studies. The activities range from those dealing with the aesthetics of the urban place (*Artists in the City*, Chapter 1) to theories of urban structure (*Using Census Information; Choropleth Profile of a City*, Chapter 21). They include opportunities to use classic theories of urban planning in simulations (*Modern Town Planning Primer: Subdivision Plan*, Chapter 34) as well as to use one's imagination in bettering urban environments (*Rooftop Design*, Chapter 29 and *Landscape Design*, Chapter 30). In addition, several of the activities deal with people's perception of the urban setting (*Ecological/Morphological Distances*, Chapter 13 and *Urban Humour*, Chapter 10) and the implications of these perceptions in marketing and planning (*Do We Need Another School?*, Chapter 18 and *Shopper Behaviour: The Principle of Least Effort*, Chapter 16.)

**Urban Toolkit** is divided into three sections:

- Section A   Urbanization
- Section B   Urban Environments
- Section C   Integrative Studies on Urban Development

While the organization of *Urban Toolkit* reflects the requirements of curricular frameworks, choices regarding the order of presentation for each activity are completely open-ended. Also, it is not expected that all of the activities need to be completed in order to fully benefit from the book. Each activity is designed to stand on its own, independently complementing and extending existing materials already in use. It is expected that teachers would select those activity topics that they feel best support their own classroom resource needs.

Activities vary in length and difficulty; however, the format within each activity is consistent for easier referencing. Each activity begins with an introduction to the topic, followed by a listing of **materials** required to complete the activity. The **preparation** stage guides the students, step-by-step through the main assignment through to a selection of thoughtful **conclusions**. Optional **further study** suggestions are incorporated with most activities for investigations beyond the scope of the main assignment.

Supplementary **blackline masters** (provided by the teacher) are required to complete some of the activities and these are clearly indicated both in the materials list and also in the margin area of the text.

Throughout the book the authors have attempted to strike a balance, presenting both the advantages and limitations of modern urban life. However some biases are inevitable—the authors like cities. It is their belief that cities are intrinsically good places in which to live and work and that the human spirit and creativity are capable of overcoming a multitude of challenges. Some of these challenges are offered here!

# Urbanization

# The Artist in the City

1

You can learn a great deal about cities through the eyes of artists. But why is this? What possible difference can there be between the way an ordinary citizen sees the city and the way an artist views the same city?

History teaches us that as cities developed they became cultural and artistic centres where people could find diversion and entertainment. Artists were drawn to these urban centres to offer their talents and crafts for the large and often wealthy audiences to be found there. And it is in the lasting works of these artists that the great pictures and stories of urban glory of the past are enjoyed by people today.

The greatness of cities celebrated in the works of famous artists has offered a model for other cities to copy and improve on. At the same time, throughout the ages, artists have also depicted the problems of urban society, which has often moved city elders to take measures to improve the quality of life in their cities. In the following activities, you will examine some of the urban visions that artists have shown us. You will also be asked to seek out some modern artists' viewpoints about cities to consider how you, as future planners of cities, can strengthen and enhance your urban environment.

## Artists' Impressions of the City

On these pages are examples of artists' works from different ages throughout history.

1. Form small groups and assign one artist's work to each group. Discuss in your group what statement you think your artist is making about the city.
2. Share your findings with the rest of the class, explaining how the city has been depicted in your group's work of art.
3. Is there any pattern of concern about city living evident in the feelings of these artists? Discuss what these concerns might be.

Figure 1.1 Metropolis, 1926. In what ways has Fritz Lang's vision of the city of the future become a reality in modern cities?

## Cities

*Think of London, a small city*
*It's dark, dark in the daytime*
*The people sleep, sleep in the daytime*
*If they want to, if they want to.*

*Chorus: I'm checking them out*
*I'm checking them out*
*I got it figured out*
*I got it figured out*
*There's good points and bad points*
*Find a city*
*Find myself a city to live in.*

*There are a lot of rich people in Birmingham*
*A lot of ghosts in a lot of houses*
*Look over there!...A dry ice factory*
*A good place to get some thinking done.*

*Down El Paso way things get pretty spread out*
*People got no idea where in the world they are*
*They go up north and come back south*
*Still got no idea where in the world they are.*

*Did I forget to mention, forget to mention Memphis*
*Home of Elvis and the ancient Greeks*
*Do I smell? I smell home cooking*
*It's only the river, it's only the river.*

**(David Byrne)**

**Figure 1.2 Acropolis. A classical urban model.**

**Figure 1.3 View of Quebec City, early 1880s. What factors contributed to make this an attractive site for a city?**

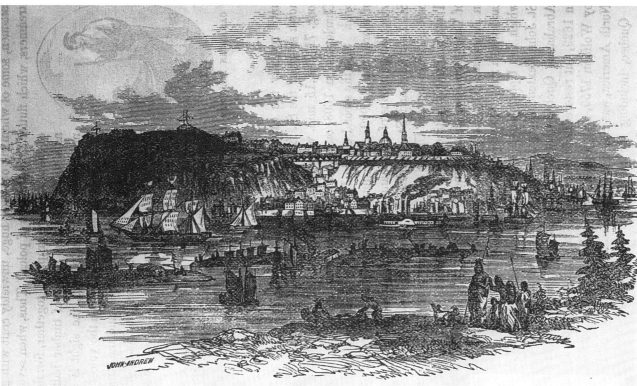

CITY OF QUEBEC.

Figure 1.4 Wall mural showing an important economic activity, Chemainus, B.C. What activity would best represent your community on a wall mural?

Figure 1.5 Sheepscape. Montreal wall design. Justify the use of such murals to enhance the appearance of drab buildings.

## The Best Street

*In the early, early morning*
*When the city is almost quiet,*
*You can go out and hear the streets speak.*
*No kidding! Just try it.*
*"I'm the best street,"*
          *You'll hear the highway say,*
*"I get them where they want to go."*
*"I'm the best street,"*
          *says Broadway,*
*"I really give them a show."*
*"I'm the best street,"*
          *says Market Street,*
*"It's here that money changes hands."*
*"I'm the best street,"*
          *says Main Street,*
*"It's I who have the marching bands."*
*"I'm the best street,"*
          *you can hear the alley say,*
*"To me come all the homeless cats and dogs*
          *that stray."*

ROVING · SPINNING · WEAVING ON A HORIZONTAL LOOM · WARPING · NURSING ·

**Figure 1.6** Egyptian tomb art. In what ways can this ancient form of communication be compared to billboards, murals, and advertising posters in depicting modern urban living?

# Researching Artists' Views

## Materials

Matrix grid *(Blackline Master 1.1)*

The purpose of this section is to examine some examples of modern singers, writers, film/video makers, and painters who, in their works, present an attitude or an impression of the urban environment as they see it.

1. Find one example of a work of art from each of these categories: a poem, a short story, a song, a music video, a feature film, and a painting or drawing.
2. Be careful to note the artist's name and the artist's general attitude toward city life.
3. Record the information on Blackline Master 1.1.
4. Using all the data assembled by the class, determine the overall attitudes of the artists in each category on the chart.
5. Compare the attitudes of your selection of artists with those you examined earlier.

## Further Study

1. Design a one-page poster to encourage the development of the city, based on what you have learned from the artists.
2. Write a poem or a song to express the feelings you have about the place where you live.
3. Organize a visual presentation to inform your classmates about the positive and /or negative aspects of urban life in Canada. Consider the inclusion of one or more of the following categories as a basis for your presentation:

   ♦ the city and the individual
   ♦ the city and families
   ♦ the city and cultural communities
   ♦ the city and minority groups

# Urbanisms

As you study and discuss the design and workings of cities, you encounter a great deal of specialized terminology. One way to remember these city terms, or "urbanisms," and what they mean is through word-picture association. One example of word-picture association for the term *urban sprawl* is shown here.

**Figure 2.1
Urban Sprawl
Sequence**.

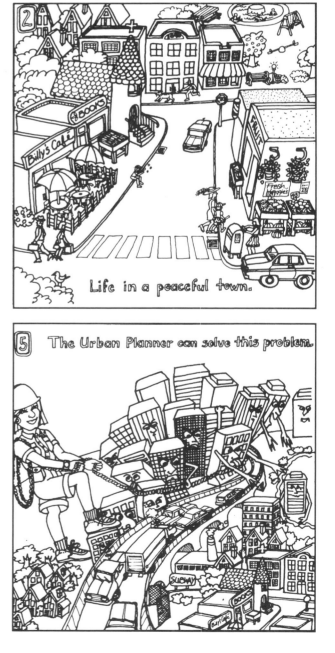

# Pictures Tell the Story

## Materials

Copy of cartoon frames sheet (*Blackline Master 2.1*)

1. Create your own personal set of picture definitions. Begin by choosing one urbanism from the list of terms below. If the word you have chosen is unfamiliar to you, then guess at a probable meaning.

   CBD (Central Business District)
   megalopolis
   peak value
   intersection
   accessibility

zoning laws
nodal regions
people space
centrifugal
blueprint plan
hamlet
landscape architecture
exurbia
rural-urban fringe
service centre
conurbation
commuter
least effort principle
urban sprawl
light industry
centripetal
break of bulk point
greenbelt
range of a good
land speculation
satellite town
spatial interaction
village
rush hour congestion
gap point
machine space

2. Compare your own definition of an urbanism to the definition defined in the glossary on pages 116-118. Adjust your definition, if required.

3. Once you have become familiar with the meaning of your selected word, use a sheet of cartoon frames to create a word-picture story such as that illustrated for "urban sprawl" (BLM 2.1). Fill in the first frame with the term you have chosen and your name. In the second frame, introduce the term, while the third, fourth, and fifth squares are used to develop a story explaining the term. In the last frame make a concluding statement. Refer back to the example on this page to clarify the sequence your picture story should follow.

## Conclusion

1. When you have completed your drawings, present your word-picture association to the class. If some of your classmates have created the same word-picture association for the same term as you, discuss how the interpretations are similar and how they are different.

2. If you wish, display your cartoon sequence in the classroom for future reference.

3. In what ways can an accurate understanding of urban terms contribute to a better understanding of how and why urban places develop?

# Perception of the Urban Place

Perception, the awareness of something through the senses, is a highly personal phenomenon. Various elements influence our perception of our environment, and not least of these is the factor of time. One's perception of an urban place may change as one grows older and the place itself may change its character over time. The Cabbagetown district of Toronto, for example, has developed from a reception area for poor working-class immigrants who grew cabbages in their front gardens to an upscale residential area in which many of the homes have been extensively renovated, a process known as gentrification.

An individual's personal experiences will affect the way that person perceives the urban place; each person draws from a personal "library" of experiences with the urban environment. Some of these will be positive: the cultural diversity of a city; the discovery of a new, previously unknown restaurant; the wide range of employment opportunities. Other experiences, such as being delayed in traffic tie-ups, the increasing incidence of crime, and the high cost of urban living may taint one's impressions of the city. Also, one's age, sex, education level, and culture will colour one's views.

In 1960, Kevin Lynch, an urban sociologist, introduced the notion of the *mental map*. This map represents the image or impression that an individual has of the spatial characteristics of a neighbourhood, an urban place, or even a province or a country. To construct a mental map, one begins with a blank piece of paper on which the individual draws his or her mental images or perceptions of the area being mapped. Often these impressions are a reflection of an individual's familiarity and experience with the area.

The following assignments involve the construction and analysis of mental maps.

**Figure 3.1 A student mental map.**

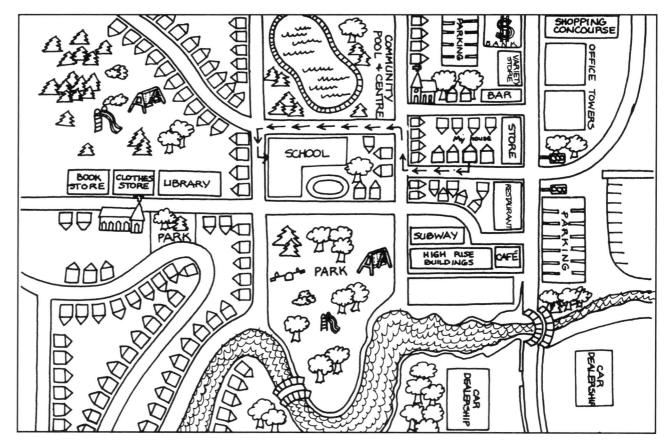

Lynch identified five interrelated elements common to most mental maps: paths, edges, districts, landmarks, and nodes.

**Paths** refer to the routes used to travel from place to place, for example, roads, sidewalks, and transit routes.

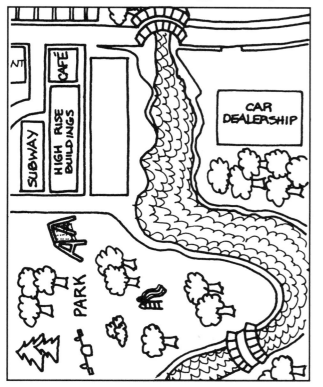

**Edges** are the boundaries—psychological and real—that one finds on the mental map. The boundaries of neighbourhoods, main streets, and rivers may appear as edges.

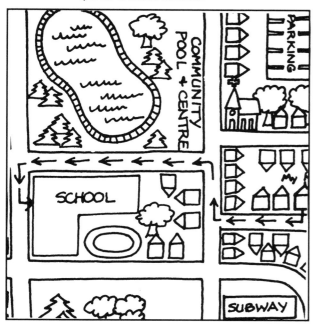

**Districts** have homogeneous characteristics that appear on the landscape of the mental map. These may be neighbourhoods, shopping districts, or any area with certain distinctive characteristics.

**Landmarks** include prominent fixtures on the landscape, such as important buildings, monuments, or other structures that serve as reference points.

**Nodes** are junctions, intersections, or meeting places. A prominent subway stop, a street intersection, or a large commercial building may serve as a node.

# Where Am I?

1. On the mental map (Figure 3.1), identify and describe at least one example of each of the five elements described by Lynch.
2. Sketch from memory a mental map of your own neighbourhood, including your home and school.
   - (a) When you have completed your map, identify and list the paths, edges, districts, nodes, and landmarks that appear on it.
   - (b) Exchange your mental map for a classmate's map and identify and list the elements found on it.
   - (c) Exchange maps between all the members of the class so that each member obtains a map drawn by an unidentified classmate. Based *only* on the information found on the mental map, write a brief character sketch of the person who made the map. *Hint:* Often what does not appear on the map can be as revealing as what is shown.
3. (a) Now that all members of your class have completed a mental map of an area familiar to everyone, display all the maps along with a topographic and street map of the area for purposes of comparison.
   - (b) Complete a matrix to summarize your findings about common and unique elements in the maps. You might use the following headings:

| Element | A<br>Elements common to at least 50% of samples | B<br>Elements common to at least 25% of samples | C<br>Elements unique to one map or appearing in less than 10% of samples |
|---|---|---|---|
|  |  |  |  |

   - (c) Explain why the elements in each of the columns appeared as often as they did.
   - (d) Why did the elements in Columns B and C appear less frequently?

## Conclusion

1. What conclusions can you reach about your class's perceptions of the area?
2. How can people's mental impressions of an area affect how they would prefer to see their city grow?
3. In what ways do your local city planners encourage development that supports your mental mapping of an area in your community? What elements would you encourage them to develop more aggressively?

# Bias—What Makes a City a Good Place to Live?

4

When you are asked where you live in Canada, how do you respond? Rather than giving a precise geographic location of your community, do you find it easier to give the name of the nearest large urban centre? For example, if you live in Blackburn Hamlet in the suburbs of Ottawa, you probably will answer that you come from Ottawa. You know that you will get an immediate response when you say Ottawa; Blackburn Hamlet would probably require further explanation. On the other hand, if

**Figure 4.1**
**St. Bazil's (sic) Church, Moscow. What arguments can be made in favour of preserving old architecture in a modern city?**

you have reason to believe that Ottawa would evoke a negative response in your questioner, you might well prefer to specify that you live in Blackburn Hamlet.

Certain images are conjured up when particular city names are mentioned. For example, what do you think of when you hear the names of these cities: Paris, New York, Moscow, Tokyo, Beirut, Rio de Janeiro, Casablanca, Shangri-la, Gotham, and the Emerald City of Oz? Each of these city names evokes a response in us. The response may be positive or negative, depending on our knowledge of that place and our feelings towards it. This activity explores the unexamined biases each and every one of us harbours toward cities.

What makes a city a good place to live? What reputation has that particular city gained over time? Some say that what really makes a good city is the pride of its inhabitants, the people who live and work there. Think of the pride you take in your urban settlement. Perhaps you would rather live somewhere else. If you had to live in another urban centre, which would it be? The following activity will help you clarify in your mind the things that popular cities have to offer.

**Figure 4.2 Travel stickers.**

# Definition of a City

If you look up the word *city* in a dictionary, you will find a definition such as the following:

> **city.** 1. a large and important town. 2. in Canada, an incorporated community with fixed boundaries that has been granted status as a city by its provincial government, usually having more financial and social responsibilities and more sources of revenue than a town. A city is the largest municipal unit and in most provinces must have a minimum population of several thousand.

Does this definition capture the spirit and vitality of the large urban centres you know about? Is there any mention of the people and special features that make a city great? To find a more meaningful concept for the word *city*, you will have to create your own personal definition.

1. On your own, begin by compiling a list of ten words that describe a city in a more meaningful way for you.
2. In groups of four, compare your lists. From these, compile a group list, eliminating any duplicates or similar words.
3. Using as few words as possible, make up a group definition from the group list.
4. Each group should write its definition on the chalkboard.
5. Look for words that are repeated in all the definitions. Have someone circle these words.
6. Identify words that are not circled but that you consider essential to the understanding of the term. Have someone underline these words.
7. Using only the circled and underlined words, develop a class definition of the city (maximum 50 words).
8. Compare your class definition with dictionary definitions. How has the definition been enriched?

# City-Shopping: Where to Live?

In what city would you choose to live if for some reason you had to move from your current place of residence? What sort of city would you try to avoid?

1. "First Choice" Cities. Choose five cities from anywhere in the world where you would like to live. Rank the cities in order from 1 to 5, with the best city first.

2. "Not a Choice" Cities. Make a list of five cities where you would not like to live. Rank these cities in order from 1 to 5, with the city you find least appealing listed first.

3. Compile a score sheet for both categories, as follows:

   First    = 5 points    Fourth = 2 points
   Second = 4 points    Fifth    = 1 point
   Third    = 3 points

4. Compile a list of the class's choices and tally the scores for each city. List the top ten choices and their scores in each category.
5. Calculate the score each received as a percentage.
6. Did any cities make both lists? Which ones?
7. Discuss how bias was involved in the choices of the cities.

# One City Versus Another

Now that you have decided on the places where you would like to live and those you would avoid, ask yourself what things made you choose these particular cities. For the benefit of future planners and decision-makers, compile a list of things you would incorporate into a "first choice" city and things you would eliminate.

1. Working in two groups, discuss and compile a list of the ten most important things your group would find attractive and useful in cities you have visited. Then agree on a group listing of the ten most common things that should be encouraged in urban planning.

2. Both groups then present their findings. What differences and similarities are there in the two groups' lists? Make revisions in your lists to reach a class consensus.

3. What strategies were used to reach a class consensus? Which was the most successful in the situation?

**Figure 4.3 Utopian City.**

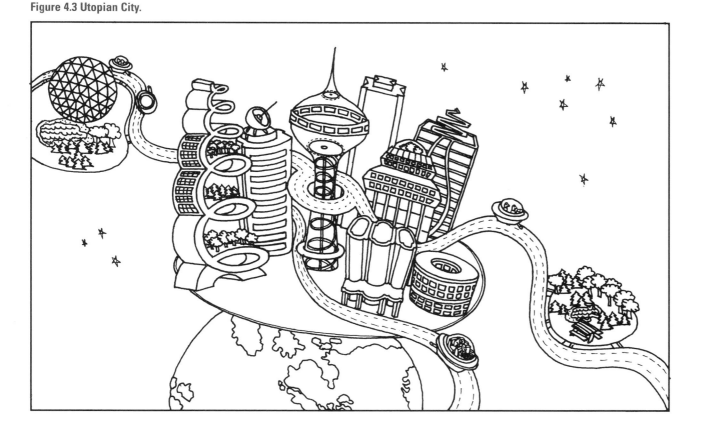

# The Changing City and the Changing Countryside

1. Consider how such things as population, size, growth, and development are changing in cities and rural areas across the country. Then create an illustration that represents your feelings and opinions about these changes. Prepare your illustration using resources such as newspapers and magazines so it can be mounted for display and discussion purposes.
2. Research and then graphically represent information to show how Canada's urban/rural population ratio has changed in the last fifty years. Compare the results of your research with population changes in your own community during the same period of time. Local reference libraries can provide you with interesting archival information about your community and its population growth.
3. What can you conclude about the urbanization of your community as it compares to that of the national profile?
4. Estimate how Canada's rate of urbanization would compare with that of other countries in the world today. How could you find out how accurate your estimate is?

# Uncovering Biases

1. What biases did you discover that you had about certain cities?
2. What biases did you discover that you had about your local urban centre? What biases did your group have?
3. What are the differences between bias and prejudice?
4. Are there advantages in city living over rural living? in rural living over city living?

## Further Study

1. Imagine that you are the owner of a very successful travel agency. Your customers are always looking for package tours that are both exotic and innovative. (Something that they can talk to their friends about for months after!)

   Prepare a brochure for a five-week tour package designed to sell your customers on a "tour of a lifetime" through

   ♦ major city centres
   ♦ ancient and old world cities
   ♦ urban centres in developing nations.

   Consider the composition of this brochure as primarily a *visual* marketing strategy—use as few words as possible. Be careful not to misrepresent any cities selected for the tour.

# Settlement Growth —A Market Town

5

A hundred years ago the economic mainstay of Canada was agriculture and most people lived in rural areas. The growth of towns can be mostly attributed to the development of service centres. These centres provided the goods and services needed by the rural inhabitants, such as machine sales and repair, groceries, household items, clothing, schools and churches, and what is most important, markets for the farmers to sell their crops. How did one town outgrow or develop faster than another? One reason appears to be accessibility. Those towns, for example, that could attract more buyers and sellers seemed to develop faster than those that were farther away or harder to get to.

In the following activity you will have an opportunity to determine the importance of accessibility by examining the accessibility of a number of settlements in the same area. From this per-

Figure 5.1 An old market town.

spective, you will be able to determine which towns are more likely to become the larger service centres.

# How Do Towns Grow?

## Materials

Base map of settlements *(Blackline Master 5.1)*

1. Determine the accessibility score for each settlement on the base map (BLM 5.1) by counting the number of roads that enter the settlement. Enter the scores on the map beside the settlement.
2. Give a name to the service town that receives the highest accessibility score.
3. Suggest three reasons why people might travel farther to buy or sell their goods in the largest service centre.
4. Of the several towns that have the second highest accessibility score, choose one that might, because of its location, attract more business from nearby smaller towns than others with the same score. Circle this more important town and give it a name.
5. Is there any pattern to the locations of the service towns on the map? Suggest reasons why.

## Conclusion

1. Select and research an ancient city of your choice. Suggest three main reasons that account for its urban growth and development. Create a chart to compare the early development patterns of this old city to those of any other large urban centre or city in the world today.

## Further Study

1. In what ways would earlier settlement growth have been affected if the economy had been based on an interactive video and information services industry?

BLM
5.1

# From Service Centre to Urban Centre

6

As you have discovered in the activity on Settlement Growth, access is one of many reasons for a town community's growth. Location, or where the community settles, is also a factor that defines and shapes a community's development. Location has two aspects: site and situation.

The site of a place refers to the physical characteristics and exact location of the community itself. For example, a town's site could be on the coast, at the junction of two rivers, in a valley, on a bay, or somewhere high up in the mountains.

The situation of a place refers to the features of the region that surrounds the specific community. For example a place's situation could be that the community is accessible by water or surrounded by mountains.

How urbanized a community eventually becomes can be determined by these location factors. Where and how a community is established can also influence the rate of growth of that community just as accessibility factors do.

In this activity you have an opportunity to access the importance of seven small urban centres in an imaginary region called Urbania based on its location factors. Using the list of site and situation factors and the base map of the region (BLM 6.1) determine which one of the seven communities will eventually become the capital city of Urbania. A matrix (BLM 6.2) has been provided to help you assemble your perceptions of each of the seven areas under consideration.

**Figure 6.1 A low level relief map.**

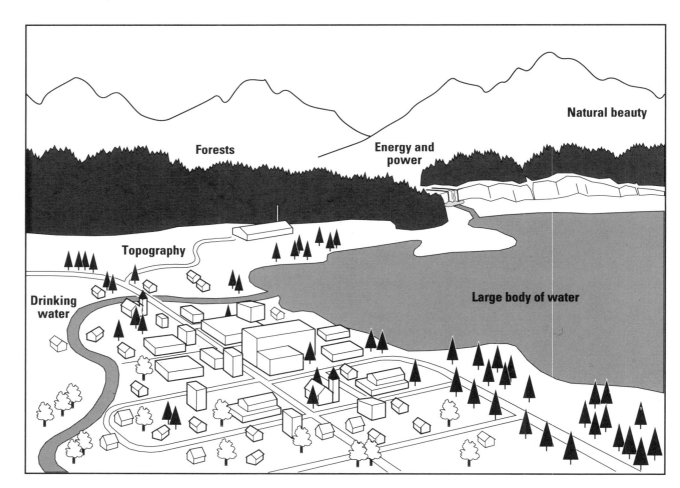

# The Emergence of a Major Urban Centre

## Materials

Base map of region of Urbania (*Blackline Master 6.1*)

Matrix to accompany the base map of Urbania (*Blackline Master 6.2*)

## Preparation

| Site Factors | Situation Factors |
|---|---|
| 1. Drinking water | 1. Navigable river |
| 2. Large body of water | 2. Access to water bodies |
| 3. Building materials | 3. Mountain pass / gap point |
| 4. Forests | 4. River confluence |
| 5. Room for future growth | 5. Bridge point |
| 6. Fertile soil / access to water | 6. Crossroad |
| 7. Safe harbour | 7. Break of bulk point |
| 8. Defensible position | 8. Trade centre |
| 9. Employment potential | 9. Regional centre |
| 10. Heating fuel | 10. Port city |
| 11. Energy and power | 11. Transportation centre |
| 12. Access to markets | 12. Foreign border access |
| 13. Natural protection | 13. Favourable climate |
| 14. Minerals | 14. International centre |
| 15. Natural beauty | 15. Political centre |
| 16. Topography | |

1. Looking at the base map (BLM 6.1) consider the needs of the people living in the area. Are the main requirements of life (food, water, and shelter) being satisfied in each settlement?

2. Each settlement has reasons for its existence, but which do you think will become the more important urban centre. In order to answer this question, fill in the base map matrix (BLM 6.2) ranking the seven possible locations. Consider all the possible site and situation factors. Some of these are obvious from the map; others may require discussion with a classmate.

   (a) Score each site factor and each situation factor on a scale of 3 to 0.

      3 = Yes          2 = Nearby/Possible
      1 = Uncertain    0 = No

   (b) Tally your score for each location.

   (c) The highest scoring city will become the new capital city. Label it on your base map.

   (d) Rank in order the remaining locations to indicate their relative urban importance.

3. Determine whether everyone is in agreement with the choice of location.

4. Suggest other factors that might influence the growth potential of an urban centre.

5. Give your new capital city a name.

## Further Study

The region has been without a capital since the mysterious destruction of the ancient city 700 years ago. Perhaps the following description of this once great city of Nineveh will provide you with clues to determine its former site. Using this description, construct a sketch of the ancient city and its surroundings. Then, using the information in the description and on the base map, determine the location of the ancient city of Nineveh. Mark the location on the map.

### Site and Situation of the Ancient City of Nineveh

Located in the raised portion of the floodplain valley at the confluence of the Rur and Urb rivers, this city was sheltered by a forest stand of oak and maple trees. The nearby rock quarries provided the city's builders with the necessary construction materials. The fastflowing river provided fresh water and power for the mills.

The sheltered harbour was deep enough for trade ships to dock. Goods were then transported up river into the city. Rich agricultural lands bordered the river. The harsh dry climate made agriculture elsewhere in the region impractical.

The city was situated on the east-west trading road at a point where the only bridge crossed the river. Nestled at the base of Mount Alexandre, this city had access to the rich minerals prevalent in the region. The only route through the mountains to the cities in the region to the north was accessible through Nineveh. The town and villages within a half-day's journey of this, the capital city, brought their goods here to market.

The ruler of these lands lived in this city because of its central location at the very heart of the country of Urbania. Within the city was the only park in the region. It was renowned for its protection of rare animals and famous for the Falls of Yowton constructed there.

In the more distant past, the settlement had been attacked by barbarians from beyond the borders of Zuza, but was successfully defended by the inhabitants. Eventually the barbarian attackers became the city's major trading partners. Most of this international business took place in this financial capital of Urbania.

# The City from Many Geographic Perspectives

## 7

Some people can find their way around in a new place without any difficulty, while others can reside in a city all their lives and still not be familiar with its layout. In this activity you will be asked to look at the city of Vancouver from several different perspectives and to decipher various kinds of visual information.

This study makes use of the following progression:

♦ an aerial photograph of the city
♦ a cartographer's interpretation of the same area features, as seen on a topographic map
♦ a street map used by people to find their way around in the city

We spend most of our lives viewing the world from ground level (horizontal view). However, when we can see our surroundings from a bird's eye view as it is seen from an aircraft (vertical view), some adjustment is required for us to understand familiar places from this new perspective. In this activity you will have the opportunity to decipher visual information from an aerial photograph. With practice you will be able to recognize and point out features that are commonplace at ground level. You may also learn to appreciate the different perspectives that planners, geographers, and engineers work with every day in their workplace.

**Figure 7.1 Aerial view of Vancouver, B.C. What site factors are easily seen from this perspective of the city?**

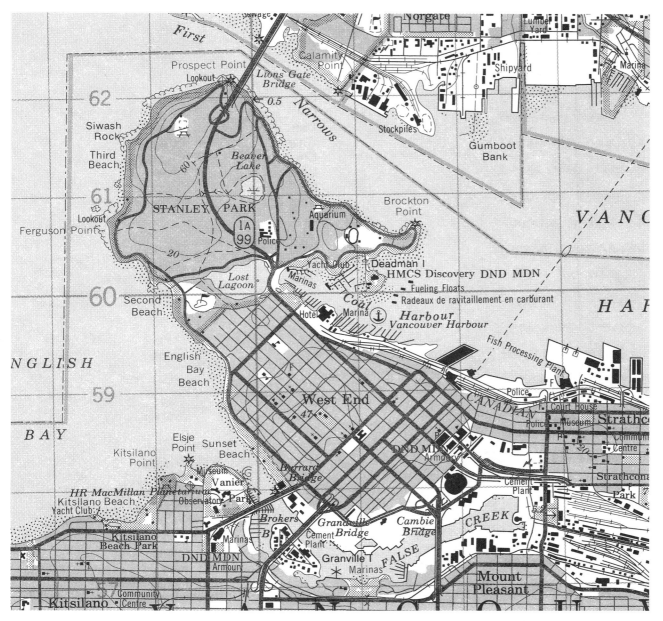

Figure 7.2
Topographical
Map system
showing a
section of
Vancouver.

# City Views

## Materials

Blue, red, yellow, black, and green pencils or pens
Base map of Vancouver *(Blackline Master 7.1)*

Complete the following drawing on the base map
provided (BLM 7.1).

1. Outline in blue the shoreline that divides the
   city from the water.
2. From information on the aerial photo and the
   maps, locate and outline in red the downtown
   core, referred to as the CBD, the Central Business District. The CBD is denoted by the cluster of tallest structures in the city.

3. With a dotted red line, outline any other clusters of tall buildings that you see.
4. Locate the main street of the city. Trace it in
   black on the base map and label it.
5. From the visuals provided, find three residential areas that differ in appearance. Locate
   them on the base map in yellow, using the
   letters A, B, and C.
6. Plot the distribution of parks on your base map
   in green.

BLM

7.1

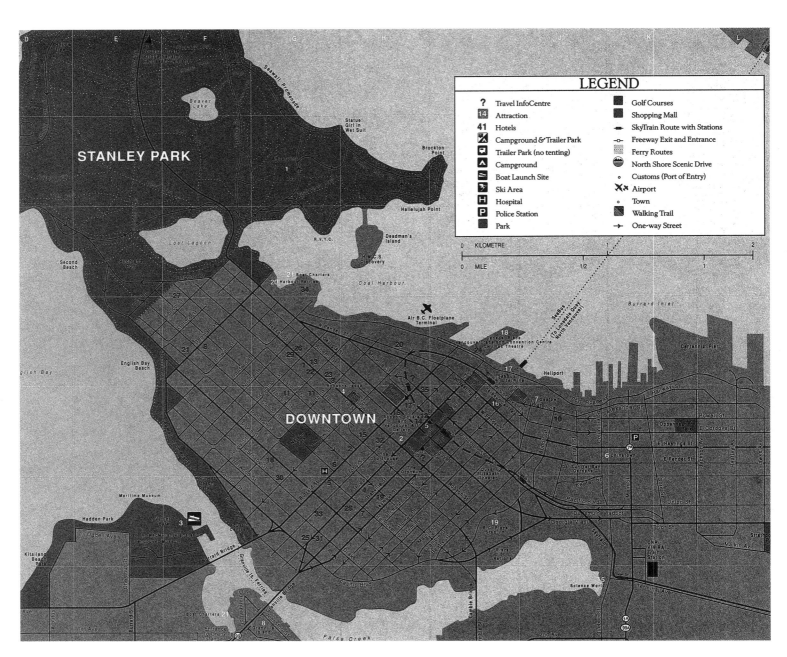

Figure 7.3 Street map of downtown Vancouver. What information can be found on this map which would be difficult to determine from a topographical map or air photo?

## Conclusion

1. Select one of the residential neighbourhoods marked on your map. Describe its advantage over other neighbourhoods.
2. How useful is it to have a number of different visual perspectives of the same area? How would you use the visual information represented on page 18 about Vancouver if you were an urban planner for the city? if you were a tourist in the city? if you were a developer in the city?
3. Comment on the amount and distribution of green space in the city.
4. Account for the pattern of tall building clusters in the city.

## Further Study

1. Study the photos of five Vancouver landmarks (Figures 7.4–7.8) and determine their location on the aerial photo and street maps of the city.
2. On your base map, indicate the location of each landmark. Use a number key, in the order you feel would be most appropriate for a tour of the city. Connect them with a line, showing the route you would follow to travel from one to the other.
3. Write a journal entry, describing a one-day tour you make to these landmark locations. Include your means of travel and the sights you see en route.

**Figure 7.4 Skytrain, Vancouver.**

**Figure 7.5 Canada Place, Vancouver.**

**Figure 7.6 View from Stanley Park, Vancouver.**

**Figure 7.7
Art Gallery
and Hotel
Vancouver.**

**Figure 7.8
Burrard Bridge,
Vancouver.**

# The 100-Year Plan
# —Building a City

8

Many cities in the world have existed for centuries and some even for thousands of years. In Canada, most of our cities are relatively young by comparison, the earliest settlements going back only to the late 1500s.

Investigations into the life of early cities reveal that these cities were faced with many of the same problems we have today: where to dispose of garbage, how to provide food and clean water for the citizens, how to make it easy for people to travel to buy and sell goods at the centre's market. These and other such concerns kept the cities to a manageable size for a long time, and the evolution of cities remained a relatively slow process. However, with the introduction of the automobile and other technologies, the city dweller had the means of travelling greater distances in a shorter time, and this allowed cities to grow to a much greater size and at a much faster rate. This multiplied the problems facing cities and made the urban planner's job one of much greater importance.

All city planners would love to have the opportunity to recreate or redesign their city from its earliest beginnings. If the early city builders had had the foresight to predict the popularity and size of the modern city, perhaps our cities would not have some of the disadvantages they do have today. One advantage of Canada's "youthful" cities is that there are fewer mistakes to be corrected by city planners than those of our older European and Asian counterparts.

Planning boards as a rule operate on a twenty year plan basis. This one hundred year plan has been invented only for the purposes of this activity.

With these thoughts in mind, you can, in this activity, begin to build a city of your own from the ground up. Working in small design teams, you will be required to make several planning decisions over different time periods in the history of your city. This simulation is not based on any particular Canadian city, but rather draws on the characteristics of many different cities. As you read along, you may recognize some of the events and features as belonging to cities you are familiar with. Your design will be in competition with others in your class to produce the best overall design.

# Building the City

## Materials

Base map of the area *(Blackline Master 8.1)*
Sheets of Mylar or tracing paper
Coloured pencils or pens

## Preparation

In laying out the plans for your city, consider the following prerequisites to the activity:

♦ Your choice of location for a noticeable focal point or city centre (CBD).

♦ Your choice of colour code and symbol chart for each land use feature in this activity. Consider universal colour/symbol codes already used in Canada. For purposes of comparison, agreeing on a common colour and symbol code for the class may prove useful at the start of each new stage of development.

♦ Your choice of five blank squares that can serve as your private property. These five squares will be evaluated at the end of the activity. Your choice is limited to those squares *outside* the 1830 town limits. Make a record of your choices on the back of your base map with an X in each of the five appropriate squares.

♦ As cities tend to cluster, consider the city boundaries of each stage of development carefully to become familiar with its size and scope. Each square represents a parcel of land.

♦ Your choice of transferring each previous stage of development onto each new map. A separate map will be required at each stage of the city's development. You may prefer to use Mylar or tracing paper overlays to display the new information at each stage or you may wish to carry forward earlier stages by redrawing.

## Stage 1: 1830

The year is 1830 and your family has lived in this settlement for 10 years. The town is a market centre for the surrounding agricultural area. It is laid out over 12 squares and occupies a total of 6 km². The focal point of the town is the Town Hall, where all the local government business takes place (city registry office, police station, fire hall, residence of the mayor). It is located on Government Square, which is indicated on the base map. Approximately 2 km west of the town (a distance of 4 squares) is the original fort. The lighthouse garrison was stationed on an island. Both are shown on the base map. Fill in the remaining land uses on the 1830 map:

♦ 2 squares: 2 churches with cemeteries and associated lands
♦ 1 square: a market centre
♦ 1 square: shops and other town services
♦ 1 square: a mill, storage and warehousing, and a blacksmith's shop
♦ 1 square: high-income residences for business and government leaders
♦ 4 squares: all other types of housing

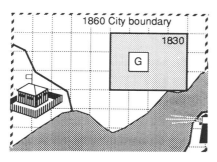

## Stage 2: 1860

The year is now 1860 and your town has been chosen as the provincial capital. As a result, 3 squares of land have been allocated for the government buildings and a park. The site chosen is located at least 3 squares away from the original Government Square, which still houses the local government. A university has also been proposed,

and 2 adjacent squares have been selected for this purpose on the outskirts of the 1830 town boundary.

Trade and commerce have grown considerably, with the lakefront commercial and service area now occupying 2 squares of lakefront land. Another 2 squares along the lakefront have been set aside for warehousing and the storage of goods from ships. Another church with a cemetery has been built on a square to the northeast of the 1830 town limit. A textile mill, a furniture factory, and a tannery occupy 1 square each. A fish plant and a distillery are well-established industries by this period, each occupying 1 square of land. The court house and jail occupy 1 square. Because of the 1834 cholera epidemic, 2 squares of existing housing had to be destroyed on the east side of the 1830 town boundary. These squares are currently vacant and will be built on during the next stage of development. The old glacial lakebed has provided a clay suitable for the manufacture of bricks, and a brickworks and brickyard have been established on 2 squares just beyond the 1860 town boundaries. Housing developments include 10 squares; 2 of these are high-income residential.

The town's population has tripled since 1830, and the town now occupies approximately 36 squares.

Fill in the land uses on your map or overlay to show the town as it existed in 1860.

## Stage 3: 1890

By 1890 the railroad has changed the shape and growth rate of the city. The railway has cut a path from the southwest corner of the base map through to the northeast corner. Draw in the railway line. The line veers into town close to the old Government Square, and 1 square has been expropriated to provide for a train station and a hotel. Developers are building in the area along these railway lines as the demand for railway access increases. Marshalling yards outside the 1890 city boundaries are used to arrange freight cars by cargo type (3 squares).

Industry has flourished, with the addition of 3 major industries occupying 1 square each. These include a brewery, a meat-packing plant, and a food-processing plant. A fairground has been opened, covering 4 squares on the west side of the city adjacent to the railroad for easy access. The annual fall fair displays the fine array of agricultural goods grown in the region.

The town has now become a city. The population has quadrupled and 20 squares are now required for housing: 5 squares are considered high-income residential, 5 squares are middle-income housing, and the remaining 10 squares, close to the factories, have been set aside for low-income housing. Some of the housing is subsidized by the industries in the city.

In anticipation of further development, 50 squares of forest land are to be cleared. The government has set aside 80 squares as Crown Land; no development will be allowed on these lands. They lie on the west side of the base map outside the 1890 boundaries. In 1871 a fire, fanned by winds from the southwest, spread rapidly throughout the predominantly wooden structures of the city. The fire destroyed the buildings on 25 squares of land immediately north and east of Government Square. They will be ripe for development in the next stage.

The city now occupies approximately 67 squares of the base map. Complete the land uses on your map or overlay to show the city in 1890.

## Stage 4: 1920

The year is 1920, and the world has just survived "the war to end all wars." The city's growth has slowed now. A coal-burning power plant and a water treatment plant have been built by the city. Each occupies 1 square of land beside the water. Coal for residential heating is stored in yards on 2 squares east of the city.

"Make work" projects, created to provide jobs during an economic depression in the area, have cleared another 20 squares of forest land outside the 1920 city limits. Industries specializing in clothing fashions and the garment trade have developed and occupy 4 squares. Reclaimed swamp land on the city's east side has been redeveloped as a port area with warehousing. Industrial expansion requires 5 more squares, either within the existing industrial area or near the new port.

The lure of the city has attracted new residents. Post-war housing for families with modest means has been constructed. Housing now requires 26 squares: 6 high-income, 10 middle-income, and 10 low-income. A new hotel district near the train station has been developed on 2 squares.

The city now occupies approximately 105 squares. Locate all the above land uses on your 1920 map or overlay of the city.

## Stage 5: 1950

It is 1950 and the Second World War has been over for five years now. The veterans are back home and at work again. In this period of the city's growth the major contributors are the "baby boom" and the increased number of automobiles. Bedroom communities are thriving on the outskirts of the city. A major east-west highway will occupy a strip half a square wide along the entire length of the base map, following the city boundary of 1950. Shade in the highway route and give the highway a suitable name.

An international airport has opened on 4 squares of land on the north side of the new highway outside the 1950 city limit. New industries are being built around the airport. They occupy 10 squares of land. A second water treatment plant has been built on 1 square, and 2 garbage dumps occupy 1 square on the east side of the city and 1 square on the west.

Commercial strip retailing is now popular. One such strip, 1 square wide, runs for a total of 10 squares in a north-south direction. A similar commercial strip runs in the east-west direction. In the area east of Government Square, 5 squares have been redesigned for commercial services. The city's first suburban shopping mall now occupies 3 squares. Housing of all types has been built in the

Figure 8.1 Toronto waterfront, circa 1930. What are the similarities and differences between the Toronto and Liverpool views?

Figure 8.2 Liverpool waterfront, England in the 1930s.

suburbs within the 1950 boundaries—90 squares in all. Of these, 20 are high-income, 50 are middle-income, and 20 are low-income. Some of the older residential areas are deteriorating, and 5 squares have already been condemned. These are available for redevelopment at the next stage.

In response to citizens' demands, 15 squares scattered throughout the city are provided for educational, religious, and recreational purposes.

The city has now reached approximately 250 squares in area. Complete the 1950 map or overlay with the above land uses.

## Stage 6: 1980

In 1980 an economic recession forced the closing of 5 squares of commercial businesses and 5 squares of inner city industries. These are available for redevelopment at a later stage. Industries have continued to leave the expensive downtown land area. Redevelopment projects and condominiums have occupied the downtown core. All the previously vacant lands in the downtown area are now occupied by the homes of the "baby boomers" of the 1950s.

A pioneer village has been planned around the old mill area. (See Stage 1: 1830–1 square.) This site has been designated a World Heritage Site.

Between 1950 and 1980 this city has experienced tremendous growth. The following features have been added:

♦ a sports stadium (4 squares)
♦ a new university on the city outskirts (4 squares)
♦ travel and tourism hotels and theatre districts in the downtown core (2 squares)
♦ 6 new suburban shopping malls (2 squares each)
♦ 3 new downtown commercial centres (2 squares each)
♦ a nuclear power plant on the lakefront (2 squares)
♦ 2 north-south highways located just east and west of the downtown core running through expropriated lands (½ square wide)
♦ a second airport (4 squares)
♦ 6 suburban industrial parks (4 squares each)
♦ a large steel plant (4 squares)
♦ a car manufacturing plant (4 squares)
♦ new police headquarters (1 square) and 7 established police stations and 7 fire halls (1 square each)

♦ a zoo (2 squares)
♦ a major theme park near a major highway (2 squares)
♦ a hospital and medical centre (1 square)
♦ new housing (75 squares in all: 15 high-income, 40 middle-income, and 20 geared to income of families)
♦ parks, schools, and churches (14 squares)

Flooding occurred recently in the river confluence area, destroying all the land uses in 20 squares. These land uses must be transferred elsewhere within the city. This area is designated as a future park.

A subway line is to be built to move the maximum number of people to the major nodes within the city as efficiently as possible. These nodes include such major gathering points as the central business district, the sports stadium, the airport, and the shopping centres. Funding is available for a maximum of 10 subway stations, covering a 20 km length (40 squares) of the system. Locate these stations.

A financial centre, including a stock exchange and the main offices of the Canadian and foreign banks, now occupies the most sought-after, and therefore most expensive, square of land in the central area of the city. At this point the city has reached a size of approximately 445 squares.

Show these revised land uses on your 1980 city map or overlay.

## Stage 7: 2010

By the year 2010 there will be 3 new satellite city centres with 1 square for the central business district in each centre (1 NE square, 1 NW square, and 1 SW square). These satellite centres will attract land development around them.

Highways will be built to connect these satellite centres with the main city centre. The subway line will also be expanded another 20 km (40 squares) and 10 new stations will be added.

The Crown land will be declared a provincial park. Give it a suitable name.

The remainder of the map can be developed however your group wishes. You are projecting the direction your city will develop in, based on the previous six stages. By the year 2010 all the squares on the base map will have been planned, and this megalopolis will occupy approximately 800 squares.

# Evaluating Your City Plan

## Part A: The "Up" Side

From a given base of 100 points, determine your overall planning score from the perspective of residential land value. Add points over and above 100 points for the following items:

1. Historic Site: Add 1 point for every residential area within 5 squares.
2. River Valley and Open Space: Add 2 points for every residential area not adjacent to but within 5 squares of the highway.
3. Access to Shopping Centres: Add 1 point for every residential area not adjacent to but within 5 squares of the shopping centre.
4. Subway Access: Add 3 points for every residential area that is within 2 squares of the line.
5. Schools and University: Add 2 points for every residential area within 4 squares of a school or the university.

## Part B: The "Down" Side

From the perspective of residential land value, determine your overall planning score. From the points already accumulated for the "Up" Side, deduct points for each of the following considerations:

1. Nuclear Power Plant: Deduct 1 point for every residential area within 5 squares of the plant.
2. Sewage and Garbage Disposal: Deduct 1 point for every residential area within 5 squares of the disposal site.
3. Sports Stadium: Deduct 1 point for every residential area within 4 squares of the stadium.
4. Shopping Centres: Deduct 1 point for every residential area within 1 square of the centres.
5. Meat Packing: Because of the prevailing winds from the west, deduct 1 point for every residential area within the following boundaries: 15 squares to the east, 5 to the north, 5 to the south, and 5 to the west.
6. Industries: For any residential area within 4 squares, deduct 1 point.
7. 1890 Fire and 1980 Flood: Deduct 1 point for every industrial or commercial square or fire or police station square affected by the fire or the flood, 2 points for every residential square affected, and 3 points for any other land use affected.

Record your score.

## Conclusion

1. Compare your score with the score of others in your class.
2. Consider the weighing system used. Would you have chosen to value points in the same way? In what ways would your own system of scoring have been different from the one used in this activity? What does this particular system of weighing reveal about the biases of its creators? If the creators of this system of points were city planners, what platform for development would they choose?
3. Remember the five blank squares that you chose as personal property at the beginning of this activity? Check the back of your base map to review their exact location. If you want to discover how valuable your property is in the new urban centre, use the land values matrix on page 27 to determine its value. Here is an example of how your property value may score.

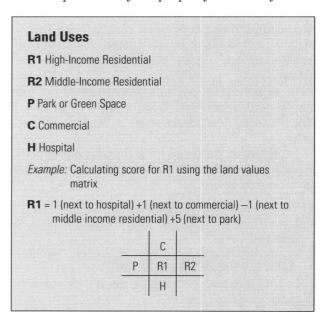

**Land Uses**

**R1** High-Income Residential

**R2** Middle-Income Residential

**P** Park or Green Space

**C** Commercial

**H** Hospital

*Example:* Calculating score for R1 using the land values matrix

**R1** = 1 (next to hospital) +1 (next to commercial) −1 (next to middle income residential) +5 (next to park)

4. Assess the compatibility of your choice of five squares with the surrounding land uses. What observations can you make about the compatibility of land uses with that of city building and development?
5. Based on your experience with small town growth in this activity, establish a set of recommendations or criteria to guide local planners with any future decisions they may have to make concerning further development in your community or neighbourhood.

# Land Values Matrix

| Some land uses are more compatible than others. Use the items listed below to calculate a score as they are affected by a location next to these uses. | Commercial services/Hosp. | Commercial-plaza | Community fire & police | Disposal-garbage/sewage | Government bldgs | Church/schools/university | Historic site | Housing-high income | Housing-middle income | Housing-low income | Industry-all types | Park-open space | Park-theme | Park-zoo | Power plant-coal | Power plant-nuclear | Sports stadium | Transport-airport | Transport-highway | Transport-railroad | Transport-train station | Water treatment |
|---|---|---|---|---|---|---|---|---|---|---|---|---|---|---|---|---|---|---|---|---|---|---|
| Commercial services/Hosp. | 0 | 2 | 0 | −5 | 4 | 3 | 4 | 1 | 2 | 3 | −5 | 1 | 1 | 1 | −4 | −4 | 2 | 2 | 5 | 0 | 3 | −2 |
| Commercial-plaza | 2 | 0 | 0 | −5 | 4 | 4 | 0 | 2 | 3 | 4 | −4 | 2 | 2 | 2 | −4 | −4 | 3 | 3 | 5 | 0 | 4 | −2 |
| Community fire & police | 1 | 2 | 0 | −3 | 2 | 2 | 3 | 3 | 2 | 2 | 4 | −2 | −2 | −2 | −4 | −4 | 4 | 3 | 2 | 0 | 2 | −2 |
| Disposal-garbage/sewage | −3 | −3 | −2 | 0 | −2 | −5 | −4 | −5 | −5 | −5 | 2 | −3 | −3 | −3 | 1 | 1 | −4 | −2 | −3 | 1 | −3 | −5 |
| Government bldgs | 2 | 2 | 1 | −5 | 0 | 2 | 2 | −3 | −2 | −2 | −3 | 4 | −3 | −3 | −4 | −4 | −2 | 4 | 3 | −4 | 2 | 0 |
| Church/schools/university | 2 | 3 | 1 | −5 | 1 | 0 | 1 | 2 | 1 | 0 | −5 | 5 | −2 | −2 | −4 | −4 | −2 | −2 | 0 | −1 | 3 | −2 |
| Historic site | 0 | −1 | −1 | −5 | 1 | 2 | 0 | 4 | 3 | 2 | −5 | 5 | 5 | 5 | −4 | −4 | −2 | −2 | 1 | −1 | 1 | −2 |
| Housing-high income | 1 | −1 | 1 | −5 | 0 | 1 | 5 | 0 | −1 | −4 | −5 | 5 | −2 | 1 | −4 | −4 | −4 | −4 | −4 | −4 | −4 | −4 |
| Housing-middle income | 2 | 1 | 1 | −5 | 0 | 2 | 5 | 5 | 0 | −1 | −5 | 5 | −2 | 1 | −4 | −4 | −3 | −4 | −4 | −4 | −2 | −3 |
| Housing-low income | 3 | 2 | 2 | −5 | 1 | 2 | 5 | 3 | 4 | 0 | −5 | 5 | −1 | 1 | −4 | −4 | −2 | −4 | −4 | −3 | 1 | −3 |
| Industry-all types | 2 | 0 | 4 | 2 | −2 | −3 | −5 | −5 | −4 | −3 | 0 | 1 | 0 | 0 | 4 | 5 | 2 | 5 | 5 | 5 | 0 | 4 |
| Park-open space | 1 | 1 | 0 | −5 | 3 | 5 | 5 | 5 | 5 | 5 | −2 | 0 | 0 | 0 | −5 | −4 | 1 | −4 | −4 | −3 | −1 | −4 |
| Park-theme | 1 | 1 | 1 | −5 | 0 | 1 | 2 | 3 | 4 | 2 | −4 | 5 | 0 | 3 | −5 | −5 | 2 | −1 | −5 | −3 | 4 | −3 |
| Park-zoo | 1 | 2 | 1 | −5 | 0 | 1 | 2 | 3 | 4 | 2 | −4 | 5 | 2 | 0 | −5 | −5 | −2 | −4 | 5 | −2 | 1 | −3 |
| Power plant-coal | 1 | 2 | 5 | 4 | 1 | 1 | 0 | 2 | 2 | 1 | 4 | 5 | 0 | 0 | 0 | 1 | 1 | 3 | 4 | 4 | 0 | 5 |
| Power plant-nuclear | 1 | 2 | 4 | 4 | 1 | 1 | 0 | 2 | 2 | 1 | 4 | 5 | 0 | 0 | 1 | 0 | 1 | 3 | 4 | 4 | 0 | 3 |
| Sports stadium | 3 | 3 | 2 | −3 | 2 | 2 | 3 | 2 | 2 | 2 | 1 | 4 | 2 | 2 | −4 | −3 | 0 | 5 | 5 | 0 | 3 | −2 |
| Transport-airport | 1 | 2 | 2 | 0 | 2 | 0 | 0 | 1 | 2 | 1 | 4 | 3 | 3 | 1 | −2 | −2 | 1 | 0 | 5 | 2 | 3 | −2 |
| Transport-highway | 2 | 3 | 2 | 1 | 2 | 2 | 2 | 1 | 1 | 1 | 2 | 0 | 2 | 2 | 2 | 2 | 2 | 3 | 0 | 1 | 1 | 1 |
| Transport-railroad | 1 | 1 | 1 | 1 | 1 | 1 | 1 | 0 | 0 | 0 | 4 | 0 | 1 | 1 | 1 | 1 | 1 | 2 | 1 | 0 | 5 | 1 |
| Transport-train station | 4 | 3 | 2 | −4 | 3 | 3 | 3 | 0 | 1 | 1 | 3 | 0 | 4 | 4 | −3 | −3 | 4 | 4 | 3 | 5 | 0 | −3 |
| Water treatment | 1 | 1 | 1 | 4 | 1 | 0 | 1 | 0 | 0 | 0 | 4 | 3 | 2 | 3 | 1 | 2 | 1 | 1 | 2 | 1 | 0 | 0 |

*Example*: The historic site beside commercial services would have 0 effect on the historic site, however, commercial services benefit in having a location beside the historic site as indicated by the +4 score.

## Further Study

1. Prepare a report to defend your city plan. Try to anticipate criticisms of your plan by outlining both the limitations as well as the benefits of its design.
2. In what ways does this entire activity illustrate the challenges of long-term planning? Find a way to graphically represent those aspects of city planning that are the most challenging.
3. Which two of the city plans would you judge to be the most successful? Are there any design similarities between them?
4. How may city development change as city planners today begin to make more informed decisions about how a city should grow?

# A Primer of Urban Architecture

9

One of the pleasures of living in an urban place is the quantity and variety of its architecture. It is in buildings that people live, work, and play. Buildings are synonymous with culture and the longevity of architectural forms attests to the fact that architecture is one of the more substantial art forms.

It is therefore almost an obligation for the urban dweller to develop an appreciation of good architecture and an awareness of poor work. This Primer summarizes and describes some of the more typical architectural styles found in urban Canada. Each style is accompanied by a brief description and a list of "indicators" that help identify the style or time period. In terms of architecture, Canada is a young nation. With the exception of Quebec City and Old Montreal, most buildings in Canada are of recent construction. This Primer deals only with styles popular after 1800.

## Making an Architectural Inventory

1. Prepare a classification of the architectural styles found in your community. Produce either an architectural map or a graphic inventory of the significant buildings located in the area chosen.
2. Find and photograph (or videotape) one example of each of the architectural styles described. If not all these styles are available in your community, look for examples in magazines and newspapers. The class may be divided into groups, with each group responsible for producing a display board of one architectural style, complete with sketches and detail photographs.

### Conclusion

1. What do the architectural presentations tell you about the historical development of your community? Create a time/sequence chart to represent your community's architectural development over the years.
2. What style of architectural development would you most like to encourage in your community? Why? Create a slogan for your city to reinforce the development you wish to maintain or encourage in your community.
3. Assess the usefulness of an architectural heritage in a community.

Georgian

1800-1870s

This was the first European style of building to be constructed in many parts of Canada. With its relatively simple, elegant lines, the Georgian style was used for both residential and public buildings.

### Indicators

- ♦ Rectangular box-like shape.
- ♦ Formal symmetry, with elaborate entrances centrally positioned.
- ♦ Hipped or gable-end roofs.
- ♦ Plain cornices and large tall chimneys.
- ♦ Windows are typically symmetrical, of the multipane tall sash type. Dormers and shutters are common.
- ♦ Brick work often consists of one colour with a different contrasting accent colour at the corners and around windows.
- ♦ Later Georgian buildings had more decorative flourishes, such as elaborate brickwork with an increased use of curves.

## Neo-Classicism
1820s-1880s

Based on the styles of the classic Greek and Roman civilizations, Neo-Classical architecture, or the Classical Revival Style (as it was also known), was particularly favoured for civic and commercial buildings where a formal and rather imposing appearance was deemed suitable.

**Indicators**

- ♦ Formal, plain, symmetrical shape with few curves.
- ♦ Use of columns and lintels. The only "soft" shapes used in this style are the cylindrical columns.
- ♦ Smooth surfaces.
- ♦ Low-pitched flat roofs.
- ♦ Wide impressive stairs leading up to the main entrance.
- ♦ Windows and doors are rectangular.

## Gothic Revival
1840s-1890s

This style, whose roots lie in medieval Europe, was popular in the Victorian Age and was used extensively in the design of churches. In residential buildings, the style is characterized by steeply pitched roofs and elaborate brick and woodwork.

**Indicators**

*In churches and commercial buildings*

- ♦ High steeples, pointed window tops, elaborate curvilinear brick-work.

*In residential applications*

- ♦ Steep roofs with extensive use of gables.
- ♦ Extensive use of tall, narrow bay windows to increase the natural light inside the building.
- ♦ Use of bargeboard or "gingerbread" wood trim.
- ♦ Decorative brick patterns and colours.

## Italianate
1840s-1880s

This is another style with its roots in Europe. A popular style for large detached residences, the Italianate Style was the Continental version of the English Gothic Style. The Italianate Style tended to model itself after the villas of southern Europe.

**Indicators**

- ♦ Light brick cladding, often with elaborate brick detailing.
- ♦ May be asymmetrical with a gable off to one side.
- ♦ Long verandas and low-pitched roofs with overhanging eaves and ornate woodwork.
- ♦ Windows have rounded arched tops.

## Renaissance Revival

1840s-1890s

This style is seen mostly in commercial and industrial buildings. Cast iron was employed extensively for decorative cornices, windows, and entrances. Sometimes, cast iron was used as a relatively inexpensive way to cover the entire façade of a building.

### Indicators

♦ Smooth cladding with elaborate cast iron detailing.
♦ Low-pitched flat roofs.
♦ Multi-storey design.
♦ Tall, round-headed windows and elaborate overhanging cornices.

## Second Empire

1880s-1890s

This style, imported from France, was very popular in Canada in the late 1800s. The most distinctive characteristic element of the Second Empire Style is the mansard roof.

### Indicators

♦ Mansard roof, often with slate or patterned shingles and dormers.
♦ Formal, square symmetrical style.
♦ Round-headed windows.
♦ Decorative details.

## Romanesque

1870s-1910s

Popular essentially as a style for churches, the Romanesque Style is characterized mainly by the use of the Roman arch for entrances and window treatments.

### Indicators

♦ Arched Roman windows and doorways.
♦ Often has asymmetrical square towers (steeple).
♦ Smooth brick cladding.

## Richardsonian Romanesque

1880s-1900

Named after the American architect Henry Hobson Richardson, this style was a distinctive version of the Romanesque Style. A rather heavy style, it was most often used for large residences and impressive public buildings.

### Indicators

- ◆ Use of red brick or sandstone for cladding.
- ◆ Can be symmetrical or asymmetrical.
- ◆ Steep high roofs.
- ◆ Use of deep arches in entranceways and deep-set windows.
- ◆ Terra cotta decoration was common.
- ◆ Massive solid appearance.

## Queen Anne

1880s-1910s

This single detached residence style, popular at the turn of the century, is described as picturesque. The asymmetric use of a multitude of details in the Queen Anne Style produces a whimsical and complicated structure.

### Indicators

- ◆ Usually light brick or cladding.
- ◆ A mix of towers, turrets, gables, bay windows, dormers, and balconies, often in the same building.
- ◆ Varied cladding materials include brick, stone, tile, and wood.
- ◆ Elaborate "gingerbread" woodwork.
- ◆ Steep gabled roofs.
- ◆ Elaborate window treatments using stained glass, arches, and a variety of shapes and sizes, often with no two windows the same.

## Late Gothic Revival

1890s-1930s

This solid, reassuring style found favour as a design for school and university buildings and churches.

### Indicators

- ◆ Similar to but less ornate than Gothic Revival buildings.
- ◆ Used in large buildings that often cover an entire city block.
- ◆ Solid, substantial appearance.

## Commercial Style
1890s-1930s

Using iron as the structural frame, the Commercial Style heralded the arrival of the skyscraper age. Purposely simple in appearance, this style reflects the idea that the function of a building should not be hidden behind an elaborate facade. The style was originally established in Chicago.

### Indicators

♦ Flat roof.
♦ Plain façade.
♦ Symmetrical windows dominate the facade.
♦ Ornamentation limited to the ground floor.

## Georgian Revival
1890s-1940s

As with many other styles, the Georgian Style reappeared from time to time in a revived or revised form. Here the style is seen chiefly in large residences or small apartment buildings.

### Indicators

♦ Most Georgian characteristics are retained.
♦ Often larger than the original Georgian Style homes.
♦ Modern additions, such as garages and conservatories, are often part of the design.

## Neo-Tudor
1890s-1940s

This picturesque style reminiscent of post-medieval England is often referred to as the English Cottage Style. Popular in many forms, the Neo-Tudor Style was widely used in the many suburbs that were developed in the first half of this century.

### Indicators

♦ Asymmetrical shape.
♦ Prominent steep-pitched roofs.
♦ Mullioned windows, often of the casement type.
♦ Use of stone on the first floor, with stucco and timber on the upper floors.

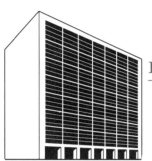

## Art Deco

1920s-1950s

The Art Deco Movement of the 1920s and 1930s produced an architectural style noted for its slick, smooth, modern appearance.

### Indicators

♦ Strong, smooth vertically and horizontally streamlined decorations.
♦ Rounded edges and glass.
♦ Use of aluminum and other metals as a trim and cladding material.
♦ Roofline setbacks in tall buildings.

## International Style

1940s-1970s

Emerging from Europe, the International Movement heralded a period in which new buildings became unornamented "skin and bones" structures (the skin being glass and the bones the skeletal frame supporting the building).

### Indicators

♦ Regular, repeated, fabricated components.
♦ Clean, unadorned appearance, often covered almost entirely with glass.
♦ Curtain-wall construction in which glass and other façade materials hang like prefabricated curtains from the frame.

## Neo-Expressionism

1950s-

This architectural movement favours unique, almost sculptural buildings that are radically different in appearance and do not fall into neat classifications.

### Indicators

♦ Use of curvilinear, free-flowing shapes.
♦ Single-purpose buildings.
♦ Mixed use of glass, concrete, and other materials.
♦ Free style.

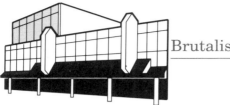

## Brutalism

Characterized by the use of raw concrete, in which the imprints of the wooden forms are left exposed, Brutalism is confined largely to large institutional buildings.

### Indicators

♦ Asymmetric.
♦ Raw concrete surfaces prominent.

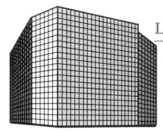

## Late-Modernism

This style takes the International Style one step further. By giving the outline of a building a less regular shape or enclosing the structure entirely in mirror glass, the Late-Modern Style attempts to personalize the repetition of the International Style.

### Indicators

♦ Mirror glass façade.
♦ Individual, sometimes whimsical, shapes.

## Post-Modernism

A reaction to Late-Modernism and the International styles, Post-Modern buildings are eclectic in their approach, that is, they borrow from a number of traditional historical styles. Combining older styles with modern materials, these buildings represent a fresh new approach to architecture.

### Indicators

♦ Forms, shapes, and ornamentation based on previous architectural traditions (arches, bays, columns).
♦ Symmetrical and formal façades.
♦ Use of modern materials with references to past styles.

# Urban Environments

# Urban Humour

## 10

Cartoonists make a living showing us the humorous side of everyday situations. However, what one person finds amusing in a cartoon may be a sensitive issue for another person. Cartoons often provide us with insights into the dilemmas of our day-to-day existence in the city.

In this activity you have an opportunity to look at ways the city is viewed through the eyes of a cartoonist. Some of the prevalent attitudes and current issues that affect our cities, as well as suggested solutions to urban problems, are presented to us every day in our local newspapers in the form of editorials and letters to the editor. However, editorial cartoons and syndicated cartoons, and even mailed-in sketches from readers, may also prove effective in putting the same ideas across.

What are the contradictions of urban life? In some cartoons, for example, everyone seems to

**Figure 10.1 What does this cartoon say about urban architecture?**

be in a great hurry to get somewhere. They can never arrive soon enough! Urban Canadians are usually described as well-behaved and well-trained in the benefits of the line-up society. Like sheep, we join long lines, sometimes not even sure what is at the other end. We laugh at jokes about smog and the poor quality of our drinking water, at exaggerations of our fast-paced lifestyle, and at the humorous solutions presented to the problems of garbage disposal sites, the high cost of rent, insufficient parking space, and galloping prices in the housing market. All of the issues in urban centres come under attack by humorists, no matter how serious the issues may be. Sometimes

humour is the only way we can get relief from the increasing complexities and absurd contradictions in urban living.

At the same time these cartoons can send us messages that prompt us into political action. People can become more aware and more concerned about issues through cartoons and make their feelings clear to the politicians and the city planners. As cartoonists continue to bring to our attention the need to address various problems of city life, we can carry their messages further through political activism and work toward changing the established attitudes of our politicians and of big business.

# Laughs in the Big City

1. Analyse the messages being communicated in the cartoon in Figure 10.1. Look at the other cartoons in this book and analyse the message in each. (See pages 6, 7, 79, and 94.)
2. Discuss alternative ways of communicating the cartoons' messages to the reader.
3. Choose a current local urban issue and draw or collect a cartoon on that topic.
4. Use your collection of cartoons about urban issues for a class display or cartoon book. The cartoons could be classified under headings such as Traffic, Housing, Urban Stress, Urban Environment, Crime, Urban Poverty, and Social Events. Add to this collection as you discover new cartoons in newspapers and magazines throughout the course of your Urban Studies.

## Conclusion

1. Are there recurring themes or topics in your assembled cartoons? Find out if this pattern is also evident with other collections in the class.
2. Form a small group and choose one urban issue. Review the cartoons collected by the members of the group and then select any relevant cartoons that are associated with this issue.
3. Compare the suggested solutions made by cartoonists with those being proposed or implemented in your local newspaper.

## Further Study

1. If you were a cartoonist, what urban issue would you feel required more media attention locally? regionally? nationally? internationally?
2. Speculate about the importance of your particular local urban concern in any third world country. Discuss your perceptions about this comparison with another classmate.

# Cemetery Study

11

P ossibly one of the more interesting insights into the history of a small community or neighbourhood is the local cemetery. Historic walking tours of city neighbourhoods often include cemeteries as part of their itinerary. The information recorded on headstones can reveal a great deal about a locality's development and the people who shaped its present form.

Pioneer burying grounds and others that date back to the earliest days of a community are generally the most interesting for analysis, particularly those that are still in use or have been until relatively recently. As well as providing a more comprehensive survey of the history of an area, a churchyard cemetery or a cemetery in a small community is more manageable for field studies.

Figure 11.1 A tombstone from the past.

In this case study, the cemetery of St. George's Church On The Hill in Islington, Ontario, is examined. The church was dedicated on October 17, 1847, and the cemetery has been in constant use since its inception. More than 2200 names are inscribed on its 713 gravestones.

# Analysis of a Burial Register

In this assignment you will have an opportunity to conduct an analysis of parts of a burial register of persons interred in the cemetery of St. George's Church On The Hill between 1847 and 1901.

1. Examine the partial burial registry of persons buried between 1847 and 1901.
   (a) Create a graph to show the range of ages of these individuals. (Persons who died before they reached the age of one year should be recorded as being one year old.) What is the average age of the individuals in this cemetery?
   (b) What conclusion can be reached about the life expectancy of people in the latter part of the nineteenth century? Why do you feel this is the case?
   (c) Is there a particular year or period of time in which a large number of people, often from the same family, died? What might this indicate?

   (d) Is there evidence that infant and child mortality rates were high? Explain why.
2. Examine the names of the people on the register.
   (a) Make a list of first names that were common in the latter part of the nineteenth century but are rarely used today.
   (b) Make a list of first names on the register that are common today.
   (c) Prepare an organizer to chart the nationality of the individuals in St. George's On The Hill.

## Further Study

1. Examine the epitaphs on the headstones of a local cemetery. Determine trends in the expression of religious feelings, sentimentality, and the sources of inspiration over time.
2. What do your observations tell you about society through time?

## PARTIAL BURIAL REGISTER 1847-1901

| Name | Age | Burial Date | Name | Age | Burial Date | Name | Age | Burial Date |
|---|---|---|---|---|---|---|---|---|
| GOLDING, Fanny | 24 yrs. | Jan. 29 1849 | BOND, Ann | 67 yrs. | July 10 1877 | THOMPSON, W. Alexander | 55 yrs. | Aug. 1 1891 |
| GOULDTHORPE, Anne | 6 yrs. | May 1 1849 | COOPER, Henry Chadwell | 71 yrs. | Sept. 12 1877 | ASHMAN, James Henry | 2 yrs. | Sept. 18 1891 |
| GAMBLE, Magdalene | 19 yrs. | Aug. 12 1849 | IDE, Charlotte | 76 yrs. | Jan. 15 1878 | ASHMAN, Mary Louisa | 5 mos. | Sept. 18 1891 |
| WILSON, William | 6 mos. | Oct. 15 1849 | WOOD, Jason Simpson | 33 yrs. | Feb. 24 1878 | BROWNRIDGE, William | 32 yrs. | Dec. 14 1891 |
| COOKE, Robert | 24 yrs. | May 9 1851 | SCOTT, William Joseph | 16 yrs. | Sept. 30 1878 | ATKINSON, Cyrelle Jesse | 5 yrs. | Nov. 3 1892 |
| COOPER, Thomas | 13 dys. | Jan. 27 1852 | FISHER, Edwin Colley | 64 yrs. | Jan. 27 1879 | CHAPMAN, William | 6 yrs. | Nov. 3 1892 |
| McCLINCHY, Mary Jane | 18 mos. | Aug. 9 1852 | YOUNG, John | 75 yrs. | Mar. 7 1880 | CARTHER, Peter | 29 yrs. | Nov. 9 1892 |
| CAMPBELL, Alexander | 58 yrs. | Dec. 11 1853 | COOK, John Albert | 2 mos. | June 15 1880 | WOOD, Charlotte Emelin | 2 mos. | Nov. 14 1892 |
| THOMPSON, William | 2 yrs. | Feb. 5 1858 | COOK, Jason Herbert | 4 mos. | Aug. 30 1880 | WOOD, Mary Josephine | 5 yrs. | Nov. 19 1892 |
| CLOUGHLY, William | 71 yrs. | Jan. 14 1859 | BROWNRIDGE, John | 46 yrs. | Dec. 31 1880 | ATKINSON, Jacob B. | 17 yrs. | Feb. 2 1893 |
| McCLINCHY, Anne | 22 yrs. | Mar. 31 1859 | TIER, Beatrice | 7 wks. | Jan. 22 1881 | WOOD, Janet | 83 yrs. | Jan. 16 1894 |
| WILSON, Jane | 43 yrs. | Nov. 30 1859 | HUGHES, John | 61 yrs. | Feb. 16 1881 | PEARDON, Everett Munro | 5 mos. | May 8 1894 |
| BROWN, Euphemia | 2 yrs. | Sept. 4 1861 | McCLINCHY, James | 73 yrs. | June 7 1881 | RHODES, William Henry | 8 mos. | May 9 1894 |
| GRIFFITHS, Joseph | 24 yrs. | Nov. 12 1862 | WOOD, Samuel | 75 yrs. | Oct. 7 1881 | PEARDON, Hazel Maude | 5 mos. | May 29 1894 |
| SMITH, Grace | 40 yrs. | Sept. 6 1863 | McCLINCHY, Emma May | 6 mos. | Feb. 3 1882 | ROSE, Sarah | 46 yrs. | Oct. 16 1894 |
| KINGDOM, Robert | 4 yrs. | Sept. 28 1863 | CLAYTON, Margaret Ann | 5 dys. | Feb. 17 1882 | SCOTT, Mary J. Peers | 43 yrs. | Oct. 16 1895 |
| JACOBS, Peter | 31 yrs. | May 30 1864 | SMITH, Georgina Ann | 17 mos. | July 24 1882 | BOND, Thomas | 44 yrs. | Apr. 14 1896 |
| MURTON, John | 49 yrs. | Aug.16 1864 | DRISCOLL, Eleanor Ida | 5 mos. | Aug. 9 1882 | WOOD, Samuel | 56 yrs. | July 1 1896 |
| CLAYTON, John | 47 yrs. | Feb. 13 1865 | McGREGOR, John | 67 yrs. | Sept. 14 1882 | COOPER, George | 54 yrs. | July 5 1896 |
| DeCOURCIER, John | 51 yrs. | June 26 1865 | KINGDOM, William | 20 yrs. | Feb. 7 1883 | BROWNRIDGE, Mary Ann | 59 yrs. | Aug. 21 1896 |
| THOMPSON, Susan Eliza | 6 mos. | Oct. 22 1865 | SCOTT, Martha | 49 yrs. | Mar. 7 1883 | GILSON, Albert | 20 yrs. | Aug. 21 1896 |
| KNOPP, Richard | 48 yrs. | July 14 1866 | BEATTY, Thomas | 57 yrs. | Dec. 28 1883 | REMNANT, Nellie | 37 yrs. | Aug. 22 1896 |
| MELLOW, Samuel | 73 yrs. | Aug. 20 1866 | MOORE, George | 71 yrs. | Feb. 28 1884 | LEWIS, Maudie | 7 yrs. | Dec. 27 1896 |
| FISHER, Sarah Maria | 41 yrs. | Mar. 14 1867 | ATKINSON, Joshua | 61 yrs. | Apr. 22 1884 | ASHMAN, Frederick Charles | 1 yr. | Jan. 6 1897 |
| MORLEY, William Seals | 35 yrs. | Aug. 22 1867 | ATKINSON, Edith Maud | 20 mos. | May 24 1884 | GRIFFITH, Margaret E. | 69 yrs. | Jan. 19 1897 |
| ATKINSON, (infant) | 6 dys. | Jan. 17 1868 | GRIFFETH (sic), James | 41 yrs. | Nov. 24 1884 | GRAHAM, Margueretta | 20 yrs. | Jan. 21 1897 |
| THOMPSON, Elizabeth | 35 yrs. | Nov. 12 1868 | SIDDALL, Henry | 56 yrs. | Dec. 18 1884 | CAMPBELL, Ludlow | 73 yrs. | Jan. 27 1897 |
| GRIFFITH, John | 78 yrs. | Nov. 23 1868 | McCLINCHY, Eliza | 73 yrs. | Apr. 3 1885 | SEELEY, John | 3 yrs. | Apr. 22 1897 |
| STALLARD, George | 17 yrs. | July 23 1869 | ELLIOTT, Robert | 34 yrs. | Apr. 27 1885 | WORGAN, Henry | 40 yrs. | May 24 1897 |
| UMPLEBY, William G. | 21 yrs. | Sept. 2 1870 | PHILLIPS, Arthur | 9 wks. | Aug. 17 1885 | BOND, Elizabeth | 14 yrs. | July 15 1897 |
| BOND, Sarah | 24 yrs. | Nov. 17 1870 | PHILLIPS, Lilly | 9 wks. | Aug. 17 1885 | MASON, Elizabeth | 27 yrs. | July 20 1897 |
| MOORE, John | 68 yrs. | Apr. 5 1872 | TOMLINSON, Charles | 70 yrs. | Nov. 25 1885 | WORGAN, Margaret Mary | 2 yrs. | Aug. 4 1897 |
| THOMPSON, Mary | 1 day | Apr. 7 1872 | FOX, Sarah Ann | 36 yrs. | Dec. 15 1885 | MEDLEY, Violet | 19 mos. | May 17 1898 |
| SMITH, Thomas | 61 yrs. | Sept. 11 1872 | SMITH, Mabel Christina | 4 yrs. | Apr. 11 1886 | MUSSON, Edward | 34 yrs. | June 4 1898 |
| BURNISTON, Elizabeth | 25 yrs. | Oct. 29 1872 | CAMPBELL, Caroline F. | 89 yrs. | July 6 1886 | PARKER, Alfred | 58 yrs. | Aug. 1 1898 |
| SIDDAL, Harriet | 40 yrs. | Nov. 7 1872 | THOMPSON, Samuel | 76 yrs. | July 9 1886 | MEDLEY, Pearl E. | 4 yrs. | Apr. 11 1899 |
| BURNISTON, Lizzy | 8 wks. | Nov. 13 1872 | ATKINSON, Julia A. | 45 yrs. | Aug. 21 1886 | MUSSON, Thomas W. | 67 yrs. | May 10 1899 |
| GRIFFITH, Alice Hall | 74 yrs. | Apr. 22 1873 | SPICER, Henry | 60 yrs. | July 31 1887 | FROST, David | 71 yrs. | Aug. 11 1899 |
| McCLINCHY, Evelyn | 11 mos. | Sept. 1 1873 | BLEA, James | 33 yrs. | Apr. 17 1888 | STRONG, Bertha | 18 yrs. | Aug. 19 1899 |
| WILSON, William | 68 yrs. | Jan. 7 1874 | FLEMING, George | 31 yrs. | Feb. 9 1889 | DUNN, Alice | 38 yrs. | Aug. 24 1899 |
| MASON, (infant) | 16 mos. | Feb. 16 1875 | CORNISH, Francis | 86 yrs. | Mar. 8 1889 | HUSTED, Silas | 41 yrs. | Oct. 23 1899 |
| ATKINSON, Ida Mary | 4 yrs. | April 11 1875 | ATKINSON, Louis Wellington | 2 mos. | Aug. 14 1889 | WATERHOUSE, Martin | 45 yrs. | Nov. 8 1899 |
| CLAYTON, Lilla | 14 yrs. | May 14 1875 | MORGAN, Richard | 33 yrs. | Sept. 29 1889 | WATERHOUSE, Mary | 47 yrs. | Nov. 15 1899 |
| IDE, Willis Aylmore | 71 yrs. | Aug. 19 1875 | OWEN, Arthur M. | 57 yrs. | Nov. 7 1889 | MEDLEY, Crelius | 28 yrs. | Nov. 16 1899 |
| GARBUTT, Emmerson | 6 mos. | Jan. 7 1876 | YOUNG, Mary Ann | 87 yrs. | Jan. 8 1890 | RICE, Ella | 17 yrs. | Sept. 19 1900 |
| BEATTY, Eleanor | 49 yrs. | Feb. 28 1876 | GILCHRIST, Harriet | 33 yrs. | Mar. 13 1890 | COOPER, Susan | 88 yrs. | Oct. 15 1900 |
| FISHER, Aylmer Hugh | 18 yrs. | Feb. 29 1876 | GILCHRIST, Harriet | 5 dys. | Mar. 13 1890 | BIRD, Margaret | 64 yrs. | Oct. 24 1900 |
| FISHER, Frances Mary | 23 yrs. | Mar. 8 1876 | VAUGHAN, Martha | 18 yrs. | May 6 1891 | | | |
| ATKINSON, David | 51 yrs. | Apr. 6 1876 | MURTON, William Alfred | 36 yrs. | July 9 1891 | | | |

# The Urban Environment —Confronting the Ecological Crisis 12

Canadians of this and the coming generation must make a profound change in the way we treat our environment if we are to maintain the quality of urban life we have enjoyed in the past. Canada used to be renowned in the world for its clean air, its abundant supplies of pure water, and its pollution-free streets, devoid of litter. This image is rapidly changing as we continue to be complacent about the deteriorating quality of our environment and procrastinate in taking the necessary actions to change the situation. Statistics present the average Canadian as a well-to-do consumer, and as one of the wealthier countries in the world, we have indeed been able to consume a great deal. Many feel we consume and waste much more than is necessary. We take for granted the goods and services we find easily available, and we continue to consume them without regard for the effects our consumption will have on the fragile environment of our planet.

More than 75% of Canadians today live in urban centres. We seem, however, oblivious of the stresses we place on our cities, and for the most part we ignore the issues that all cities must deal with. For example, we are too little concerned about what happens to the cast-off materials and waste products we produce. Garbage is not a pretty sight, and the problems it presents have often been overlooked or avoided by the urban dweller. We are great consumers but very poor environmentalists. Urban environmental issues in Canada have only recently been a priority of urban planners. We can learn from the downfall of great cities in the past what we must do to design cities in a more environmentally sensitive way. The size of successful ancient cities, for example, was determined not only by their ability to provide the necessities of life for their inhabitants but also by their ability to dispose of their sewage and refuse.

**Figure 12.1 Earth Day poster. How can you celebrate Earth Day every day?**

## Environment Report 1989

Canada has traditionally been one of the worlds' largest per capita producers of greenhouse gases that directly contribute to the warming of the planet; over 50% of the acid rain that has affected Eastern Canada has been generated within Canadian borders; over 30% of Canadian urban sewage is dumped untreated into our waterways and the St. Lawrence River is so polluted that the St. Lawrence beluga whale has been described by one scientist as the "most polluted mammal on earth."

**Source:** *1990 The Canadian Almanac and Book of Facts*

Today's cities are larger in size and have greater demands placed on them by their citizens. The Recycling Council of Ontario estimates that Canadians produce half a tonne of residential garbage a year. Most of the demands made on the city's energy and garbage systems are dealt with through services paid by tax dollars. With a flush or twist-tie garbage bag we can say goodbye to our refuse. The sewage is piped away and the garbage bags are collected right from our doorsteps. More than 90% of Canadian garbage is trucked to landfill sites. As taxpayers, we may complain about the costs, but, in reality, we may have been getting off very easy. The garbage may disappear from our doorsteps, but the challenge of finding a way of disposing of garbage has not. You may not be able to see or smell the garbage, but the garbage is still around somewhere. In some cases, garbage sites are now being sought in other communities on the urban fringe.

How can we deal with the piles of garbage we produce every day? In this activity you will have an opportunity to examine some strategies for waste management in the city.

Figure 12.2 Feed blue cartoon. Blue recycling boxes are common in many Canadian cities.

# Where Can We Put It?

1. Where were the original dump sites for solid waste and garbage in pioneer Canada? Where are the garbage dumps for your urban centre today? Where will future sites be located? What do you think about the plan to dispose of waste in outside communities?
2. Some smaller communities are prepared to take garbage from the larger centres because the larger centres are willing to pay for its removal. Find out what the going rate is to dispose of garbage from a large urban centre.
3. To what uses have old dump sites been put once they have been filled up? Research some local area dump sites that have undergone redevelopment or might be redeveloped in the future.
4. Those who manage dump sites are now becoming more selective about what can and cannot be dumped there. Some sites still accept anything. Find out what is acceptable in your local dump site.
5. How are dump sites designed? Study the design of a local dump site. What recommendations would you make to your local city planner about this site?

6. Where are sewage treatment plants located in your community? How do they work? How long have they existed in your urban settlement?
7. Construct a chronological chart to show the expansion of sewer systems in your community.

8. What can be done with the toxic wastes we produce? What are they? How should they be dealt with? Is it necessary for us to produce them? Are there alternatives to their use? Create an organizer to record your findings.

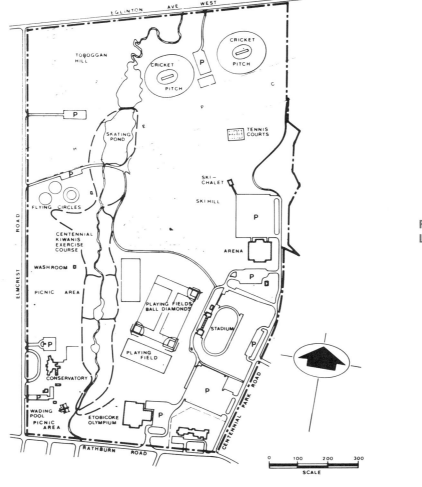

**Figure 12.3**
**Landfill site.**

## What Can We do?

1. Form small groups and brainstorm ways to actively promote environmentally sensitive issues in your community. Time limit: three to five minutes.
2. Take a survey in your community asking people to rank in order the top five environmental issues that most concern them and their suggestions for addressing these issues at a local level. Find a way to inform people in your community about the results of your survey. Inform your local city/town planners also.
3. What is your school community doing to show that it is becoming more environmentally sensitive? Initiate a plan of action to encourage and/or improve your school's involvement in such an activity.

## Further Study

1. Prepare a chart comparing the pollution indexes for various cities around the world. How is air, noise, and water pollution measured?
2. If you were to set one achievable environmental goal for yourself this year, what would that goal be? Print that goal on a small index card. Post it on a bulletin board alongside those of your classmates. Let others know that you have decided to make that goal a part of your lifestyle by signing your index card.

# Ecological/Morphological Distances

# 13

The study of mobility in urban places often deals merely with the **morphological distances** involved. The **morphology** of an urban place is the form and structure seen in its street patterns, land use patterns, relative locations, and actual distances to be travelled. The morphological distances between places can be clearly observed on maps. By using the scale provided on the map, one can determine the exact distance in kilometres between two places.

In the 1920s and 1930s, a group of urban sociologists, including Robert E. Park, Ernest W. Burgess, and Louis Wirth, working in Chicago, developed the concept of **human ecology**. These scholars, known as the *Chicago School*, were less interested in urban form or morphology than in the role the urban environment plays in shaping human behaviour. Social organization and human behaviour in the urban environment became the focus of their work. In transcending urban morphology, the study of ecology opened a whole new way of looking at the urban place.

Perhaps nowhere is the difference between urban ecology and morphology more apparent than with respect to distance. Whereas morphological distance deals strictly with the actual physical distance travelled, **ecological distance** concerns itself with the time and effort required to travel between two points. The individual's attitude or the notion of "psychological distance" is considered more important than the distance itself.

In Figure 13.1, the factory at C is 20 min by subway from the central business district. The middle-income residential area at A is 30 min away by subway. The upper-income residential area at B, which is not served by the subway, is 40 min from the central business district by automobile via an expressway. The actual physical location of the upper-income residential area is closer to the central business district, but ecologically it is farther away.

**Chicago School:** This name was given to the group of faculty and graduate students at the University of Chicago who in the 1920s developed the concept of human ecology within the larger framework of urban sociology. The pioneering efforts of these scholars helped to redefine attitudes about human behaviour in the urban setting and to focus attention on previously poorly understood ecological principles.

**Human Ecology:** is that division of urban sociology that examines human populations with reference to physical environment, cultural characteristics, and spatial distribution. Its application in urban geography often deals with how individuals perceive distance, relative location, and mobility.

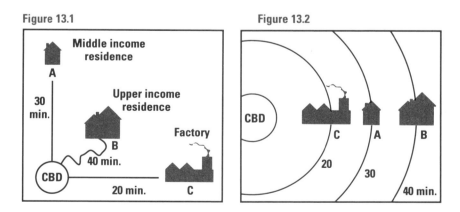

**Figure 13.1**

**Figure 13.2**

If the map were to be redrawn strictly on ecological terms, as in Figure 13.2, it can be seen that the factory is closest to the CBD, followed by the middle-income residential area, and the upper-income residential area is farthest away.

# Assessing Ecological Distance

## Materials

Matrix organizer

## Preparation

The following descriptions represent hypothetical trips made between points on Figure 13.3.

### ◆Trip #1

A commuter travels in her automobile between her home at B to her job at A. The journey takes her on the expressway. She travels with the traffic and arrives in 25 min. The total distance travelled is 20 km.

### ◆Trip #2

A colleague travels by car from his home at C to his job at A. The journey involves heavy, stop-and-go traffic conditions, with traffic lights at each major intersection. The 5 km journey takes 20 min.

### ◆Trip #3

A student travels from his home at D to his school located at E. The journey is made by taking a city bus to the subway station at F. After a 5 min wait at the bus stop, the bus arrives. The bus is crowded and offers standing room only. Stopping at every intersection, the journey to F takes 17 min. After transferring to a subway car the trip takes a further 15 min. The total distance travelled is 20 km.

### ◆Trip #4

A fellow student living at G walks 2 km to the subway stop at H. The walk takes her 15 min. The subway trip to school at E takes a further 5 min. The total distance travelled is 7 km.

1. Use a matrix similar to the one shown here to summarize the four journeys described:

| Journey | Total Distance Travelled (morphological distance) | Total Time Required | Ecological Considerations (time, effort) |
|---------|---------|---------|---------|
| #1 | | | |
| #2 | | | |
| #3 | | | |
| #4 | | | |

2. Which of the four trips is the shortest from an ecological point of view? Discuss your answer.
3. Which of the four trips would you consider the longest from an ecological point of view? Discuss.

## Conclusion

1. Conduct a field study to record the ecological distance considerations of your neighbours. Restrict your study to ten households. Work with classmates who live in your neighbourhood to compile an even larger profile of the patterns in that area. What can you conclude about your findings?
2. How does knowing about ecological distances influence developers? city planners?
3. In what ways can ecological considerations in commuters' lives affect their attitudes about urban living? What are the variables?
4. In what cities in North America do you think the issues concerning ecological distances would be the most pressing? Why?

**Figure 13.3**

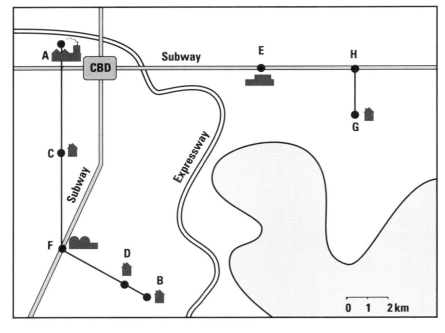

# Barriers Within the City 14

## Part A: Physical Barriers

On a daily basis we take a great deal for granted in our lives. Most of us go about our business in the city and only consider our health and our routines when they are suddenly changed in some way. For many people, particularly those who are disabled or elderly, going about one's business in the city is not so simple, for the growing city creates many barriers to their mobility. Urban planners are more aware today of the barriers urban centres present for some people in the community and are making efforts to eliminate many of these barriers. Each day the need for further change becomes more apparent as we become more sensitive to the problems of mobility some people face. Moreover, with the aging of the Canadian population, it is becoming increasingly important for planners to consider those barriers that make the city inaccessible to many of its citizens.

Every time we have to open a door, step up or down from a curb, cross a street, climb a stair, board a bus or a train or a subway, we must overcome a barrier. As long as we have no physical or age disability, there is no cause for concern, but if we are physically challenged, either permanently or temporarily, our mobility is blocked by these barriers, and we are more likely to search for ways to remove them.

## Getting Around in the City

In this activity you will have an opportunity to examine the physical barriers that affect mobility in your community.

1. Compile accessibility studies for the following trips within your community:
   (a) Home to school
   (b) Home to shopping
   (c) Home to a special function (for example, a sports event, church, the airport)
   (d) Home to a theatre or restaurant

Each accessibility study will require a sketch map that indicates the main structures of the area and the locations of all barriers. Use the symbols provided in the rating table.

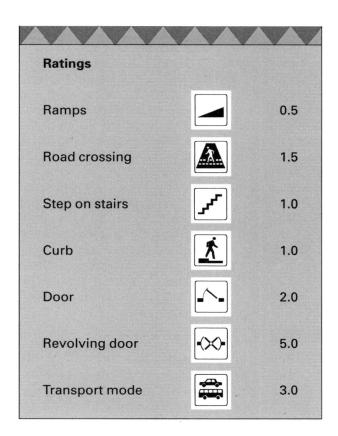

| Ratings | | |
|---|---|---|
| Ramps | | 0.5 |
| Road crossing | | 1.5 |
| Step on stairs | | 1.0 |
| Curb | | 1.0 |
| Door | | 2.0 |
| Revolving door | | 5.0 |
| Transport mode | | 3.0 |

## Part B: Invisible Barriers

Figure 14.1
"Monster
homes."

Not as readily apparent, yet just as important, are the invisible barriers that are social, economic, and cultural in nature. These barriers of even more far-reaching significance exist in any city. Natural barriers are more apparent than barriers to social and economic mobility and political and cultural barriers. As a result they are often overlooked. If not considered, these further barriers create pockets of disadvantaged citizens. Creative planners, politicians, and concerned citizens often focus our attention on these barriers in the hope that public concern will demand they be addressed when planning. Modern city planners are looking for new solutions to the elimination of these invisible barriers.

City planning in the past failed to take these social and political barriers into account, with the result that slum areas and socio-economic barriers were created. For instance, if all subsidized low-income housing is concentrated in one area, you isolate this area and create a ghetto.

This does not apply to the kind of cultural enclaves that people sometimes choose to create, as in Chinatown or Little Italy. These ethnic concentrations give colour, energy, and status to the multicultural, cosmopolitan image of a city. Such enclaves are freely chosen by the group.

Well considered long-range planning can provide a more balanced socio-economic residential design. The idea of mixing high-income, and low-income housing in the same residential development is an attempt to minimize these barriers and avoid the growth of those slum areas that are typical of many large urban centres. Planners are always open to suggestions and new ideas for removing barriers to mobility in their cities.

### Examining Other Barriers

1. In many areas so-called "monster homes" are creating pressures on their middle-income and low-income neighbours. What social, economic, and political barriers may result?

2. What barriers are being formed by the trend toward the construction of luxury condominiums, especially in the downtown core, as opposed to moderately priced, functional condominiums? Why do developers prefer to build luxury condominiums?

3. What barriers are forming in new housing projects because of price differentials and locational values?

4. What barriers are created by the high cost of living in the city? What kind of workers could be forced out of the city as a result? Explain your rationale.

### Further Study

1. Choose a physical, social, economic, political, or cultural barrier that is most relevant to you. Create a collage of messages to show how the print media and advertising can present conflicting views about this city barrier. Use articles, headlines, maps, and pictures from such sources as magazines, newspapers, travel brochures, and real estate guides to make your point.

### Conclusion

1. What steps has your urban centre taken in order to overcome urban barriers? Find an example of a barrier that has been eliminated (your choice of category) and discuss the resulting effects on the community.

2. Interview someone who is physically challenged to find out what physical barriers exist within the city. Share the results of your interview with the local planning office in your area.

3. What is the relationship between the barriers discussed and other urban issues such as poverty, crime, and homelessness? Investigate information sources such as those provided by Statistics Canada publications and INFO GLOBE to support your position.

# Interaction Between Urban Places 15

ach urban place has a *hinterland* or area that it serves. Such indicators as newspaper circulation, the frequency of telephone calls, school and commuter catchment areas, and the delivery areas of retail businesses and services are useful in determining the areas served by an urban place. However, these indicators are limited in that each accounts for only one specific aspect of consumer behaviour.

A more general and more useful method of measuring the interaction between two urban places is **Reilly's Law of Retail Gravitation**. This method is a variation of the *gravity model*, which reflects the retail consumer's attitude that "distance discourages and size attracts."

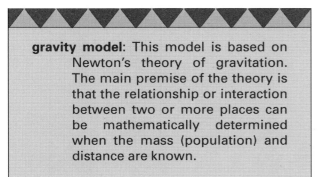

**hinterland**: This term refers to the area around an urban place that depends on the urban place for goods and services. This peripheral region varies in size. Its area is usually determined by the size of the urban place itself and the nature of the good or service in question.

**gravity model**: This model is based on Newton's theory of gravitation. The main premise of the theory is that the relationship or interaction between two or more places can be mathematically determined when the mass (population) and distance are known.

This notion can be seen clearly in the case of large, easily accessible shopping malls throughout the country. Consumers are more likely to bypass smaller plazas and malls to shop at large malls located on multilane highways. The time taken to travel to the larger mall may in fact be less than that needed to negotiate one's way through the local arterial traffic to the smaller outlets.

Reilly's Law of Retail Gravitation is a formula that allows us to estimate the retail boundary between two urban places, A and B, as follows:

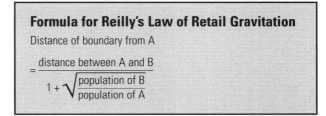

**Formula for Reilly's Law of Retail Gravitation**

Distance of boundary from A

$$= \frac{\text{distance between A and B}}{1 + \sqrt{\dfrac{\text{population of B}}{\text{population of A}}}}$$

*Example:*
The hamlet of St. Anne (population 225) is 18 km from the village of Datima, which has a population of 900. To find the distance from which St. Anne can expect to draw retail customers from the direction of Datima), the calculation would be made as follows:

Distance of hinterland boundary from St. Anne

$$= \frac{18 \text{ km (distance from St. Anne to Datima)}}{1 + \sqrt{\dfrac{900 \text{ (population of Datima)}}{225 \text{ (population of St. Anne)}}}}$$

$$= \frac{18}{1 + \sqrt{4}}$$

$$= \frac{18}{3}$$

$$= 6 \text{ km}$$

St. Anne can expect to draw retail customers from a distance of 6 km.

# Calculating Retail Boundaries

1. (a) For each of the cases below, calculate the retail boundary from A using Reilly's Law of Retail Gravitation:

| Population of A | Population of B | Distance A to B |
|---|---|---|
| 3 000 | 10 000 | 20 km |
| 2 000 | 8 000 | 12 km |
| 1 000 | 25 000 | 12 km |
| 5 000 | 30 000 | 10 km |
| 150 000 | 10 000 | 10 km |

   (b) Using a line in your notebook to represent the distance between A and B, show the retail boundary calculated above. Use a scale of 1 cm to 1 km.

2. Explain what is meant by "distance discourages and size attracts." Use local examples to illustrate your answer.

# Shopper Behaviour— The Principle of Least Effort

# 16

*"Each consumer can be thought of as having his own, highly personalized behaviour space, the extent of which will depend primarily on his level of mobility and attitude to space."*

Consumer behaviour with respect to shopping trips is of considerable interest to urban geographers, sociologists, and economic planners. Aside from the obvious economic implications of consumer spending, the spatial patterns of shopping facilities and the sociological factors that determine these patterns are reflections of the society in which we live.

The urban geographer's main interests lie in the analysis of the existing distribution of shops and shopping centres and the planning of new facilities. Of concern to them are the traffic flows generated by shopping trips, the size and distribution of shopping facilities, and the graphic depiction of this information.

Economic planners utilize much of the geographer's data to determine the financial viability of proposed shopping centres and individual retail outlets. By assessing existing patterns of consumption, the desirability of new developments can be tabulated and recommendations can be made.

The motivation and the behaviour and space perceptions of consumers can largely determine the success or failure of retail operations. Consumers attitudes are not always entirely rational, and often social factors may be more important than economic factors in determining shopper preferences. For example, an attractive small shopping mall with quality designer shops and high prices may be preferred by shoppers to a larger, unattractive mall with lower-priced merchandise.

Until recently, geographers, who are largely concerned with spatial arrangements and distance, attempted to explain shopping behaviour from this rather narrow perspective. G. K. Zipf, for example, in his *Principle of Least Effort* in 1949, suggested that the main objective of the consumer was to minimize the distance to be travelled.

**Principle of Least Effort:** This principle states that people will, by nature, attempt to plan their lives in such a way as to minimize inconveniences in distance, cost, and time.

However consumers are not only concerned with minimizing distance, and although cutting down on the distance and the effort expended are important considerations, they are by no means the only factors involved in planning a shopping trip. Among other factors affecting the consumer's planning are:

1. The nature of the good being sought. Is it a *high order good* or a *low order good*?

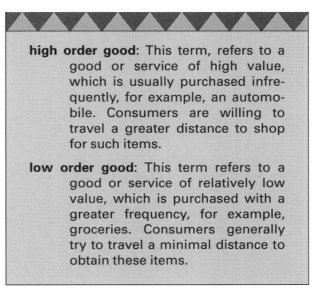

**high order good**: This term, refers to a good or service of high value, which is usually purchased infrequently, for example, an automobile. Consumers are willing to travel a greater distance to shop for such items.

**low order good**: This term refers to a good or service of relatively low value, which is purchased with a greater frequency, for example, groceries. Consumers generally try to travel a minimal distance to obtain these items.

2. The perceived attractiveness of the shopping facility.
3. Individual travel habits and experiences.
4. The number of different types of item to be purchased.
5. The shopper's knowledge of the location of retail outlets.

Clearly, distance considerations alone are not sufficient to predict and anticipate consumer movements with any degree of accuracy. When one considers that many shopping trips are of a multipurpose nature, that is, the purchase of a variety of high, middle, and low order goods that could not normally be purchased at a single store, it becomes obvious that the assumption that distance alone can determine the destination of a shopping trip is inadequate.

D. L. Huff (1962), developed a probability model that can be used to predict the probability of a consumer making purchases at a given shopping facility. In addition to the distance that must be travelled to a shopping centre, Huff takes into account the attractiveness of the centre. Attractiveness can be measured in a number of ways, although these may not necessarily be attractions that are readily apparent to the consumer. For example, the number of shops in a town or in a shopping centre can be used as an indicator of attractiveness—the more stores there are, the higher the attraction. Other indicators of attractiveness include the number of employees, the rent paid for retail space, the ground area of the retail development, and the size of the town. In each of these indicators, the higher the values the greater the attractiveness. For example, a shopping area with a large number of stores will be more attractive to a consumer looking for a selection than a smaller area. Distance in Huff's model may be measured in kilometres or in terms of time and cost.

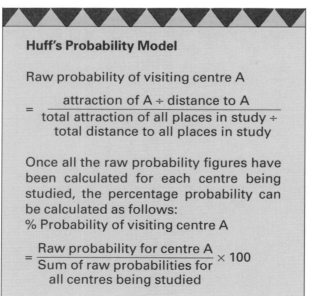

**Huff's Probability Model**

Raw probability of visiting centre A

$$= \frac{\text{attraction of A} \div \text{distance to A}}{\text{total attraction of all places in study} \div \text{total distance to all places in study}}$$

Once all the raw probability figures have been calculated for each centre being studied, the percentage probability can be calculated as follows:

% Probability of visiting centre A

$$= \frac{\text{Raw probability for centre A}}{\text{Sum of raw probabilities for all centres being studied}} \times 100$$

*Example*: The following shopping facilities are available to a consumer:

|  | Number of Shops | Distance from Consumer's Home |
|---|---|---|
| Cherry Creek Mall | 25 | 2 km |
| Gristmill Place | 20 | 5 km |
| Ashwood Village Centre | 45 | 9 km |
| Elmview Mews | 56 | 8 km |
| Maple Grove Galleria | 80 | 16 km |
| Total | 226 | 40 km |

Using the number of shops at each location as the measure of attractiveness, the percentage probability for our hypothetical consumer visiting each of these retail facilities can be determined. Applying the Huff Formula to Gristmill Place, the raw probability would be:

Raw probability of consumer visiting Gristmill Place

$$= \frac{20 \left(\begin{array}{l}\text{Attraction of}\\\text{Gristmill Place}\end{array}\right) \div 5 \left(\begin{array}{l}\text{Distance to}\\\text{Gristmill Place}\end{array}\right)}{226 \left(\begin{array}{l}\text{Total shops at}\\\text{all centres}\end{array}\right) \div 40 \left(\begin{array}{l}\text{Total distance}\\\text{to all centres}\end{array}\right)}$$

$$= \frac{4}{5.65}$$

$$= 0.7079$$

The raw probability figures for the other shopping facilities using the Huff Formula are as follows:

| Cherry Creek Mall | 2.2123 |
|---|---|
| Ashwood Village Centre | 0.8849 |
| Elmview Mews | 1.2389 |
| Maple Grove Galleria | 0.8849 |
| Gristmill Place | 0.7079 |
| Total | 5.9289 |

Once the raw probability figures have been calculated, percentage probability figures can be determined. The example again is for Gristmill Place:

% Probability of consumer visiting Gristmill Place

$$= \frac{0.7079 \left(\begin{array}{l}\text{Raw probability for}\\\text{Gristmill Place}\end{array}\right)}{5.9289 \left(\begin{array}{l}\text{Sum of raw probabilities}\\\text{for all shopping facilities}\end{array}\right)} \times 100$$

$$= 11.9\%$$

There is an 11.9% probability that the consumer in our hypothetical example will visit Gristmill Place. The probability of the shopper visiting the other four shopping facilities can be calculated using the same method. The percentage probability figures obtained in this way are useful for purposes of comparison.

# Retail Market Case Study

## Materials

Outline maps of Cambridge showing the location of shopping malls (*Blackline Masters 16.1, 16.2, 16.3, 16.4*)

Table of Major Shopping Malls in the City of Cambridge

In this assignment you will use Huff's Probability Model to determine the attraction of various shopping malls in Cambridge, Ontario. The indicator of attractiveness used will be the floor area of the developments.

### Major Shopping Malls in the City of Cambridge

| Name/Location | Level | Existing m² |
|---|---|---|
| HOME INTERIORS PROMENADE<br>Hwy. 24 and Hwy. 401 | Community | 19 840 |
| JOHN GALT CENTRE<br>Hespeler Rd. at Dunbar | Community | 17 695 |
| SOUTH CAMBRIDGE CENTRE<br>Main and Dundas | Neighbourhood | 14 779 |
| HIGHLAND PLAZA<br>Main and Dundas | Neighbourhood | 12 212 |
| THE MALL<br>Main and Shade St. | | 10 688 |
| BISHOP GATE MALL<br>Hespeler Rd. and<br>Bishop St. N. Hwy. 24 | Neighbourhood | 4 266 |
| WESTGATE PLAZA 1 & 2<br>Cedar St. | Neighbourhood | 3 642 |
| EAST-KING PLAZA<br>King St. E., Preston | Local | 2 980 |
| NORTHVIEW PLAZA<br>Glamis·Rd./Elgin St., N. | Local | 3 252 |
| PARK PLAZA<br>Dundas and Beverley | Local | 2 973 |

1. A chain of retail stores specializing in high-priced lines of quality electronics has retained your services as a consultant to determine in which of the malls the chain should lease space to open a new store. The target group of consumers for this study are those who live in grid square E4.
   (a) Determine the most direct route, by road, from the centre of grid square E4 to each of the shopping centres.
   (b) Calculate the distance to each of the malls from the centre of E4.
   (c) Using Huff's Probability Model, calculate the probability of a consumer from E4 visiting each of the shopping malls. The floor area information is shown in the table of Major Shopping Malls in the City of Cambridge.

BLM

16.1

16.2

16.3

16.4

## Conclusion

1. In which of the shopping malls would you recommend the chain establish the retail store? Give reasons to support your decision.
2. Are there limitations associated with the Huff Probability Model in a study of this kind? Explain.
3. How useful was the Huff Model in reaching the conclusion in your study? how suitable?
4. What other considerations might need to be included before a final conclusion can be reached? Would the use of the Huff Model be appropriate in assessing these considerations?

## Further Study

1. Investigate the use of a computer in applying the Huff model.

# The Dynamics of a Shopping Mall

ncreased amounts of leisure time and larger disposable incomes, coupled with the notion of shopping as a form of entertainment, have contributed to the success of the one-stop shopping mall. The convenience of the mall and its appeal as a form of entertainment have drawn consumers away from the traditional downtown shopping areas.

Typically, a large mall will have two or more "anchor" stores. These are large, nationally known department stores, which are usually located at either end of the mall. Some of the traffic flow between the anchor stores is captured by the smaller stores along the mall. Although each attracts customers for different reasons, the anchors and the smaller stores complement each other.

The planning, layout, and aesthetic appeal of a mall will have as great an impact on its success as the actual shops found in the mall.

Many small suburban plazas have undergone extensive renovations, including enclosing stores previously exposed to the weather, in an attempt to keep up with the large regional malls.

---

**Features Employed by Designers to Make Malls Attractive**

♦ An extensive use of skylights to admit attractive natural light and to create the illusion of space.

♦ The use of colour in masonry and trim.

♦ Theme gardens, courts, and areas within the mall. Floor plans that force the shopper to change direction from time to time, presenting the shopper with new vistas, are incorporated to maintain visual interest.

♦ The extensive use of indoor landscaping to "soften" the otherwise "hard," artificial surfaces of the shopping environment.

---

**Figure 17.1 A modern shopping mall.**

New malls incorporate the latest architectural motifs, designs, and colours in order to attract consumers. The use of the Post–Modern style of architecture with its historical references and typical yellow brick and green trim and glazing is currently in vogue.

In this activity you will be asked to analyse the floor plan, traffic flow, and "land use" of a large regional shopping mall, and to design a similar mall using your own creative input. You will also analyse and rank your neighbourhood, community, and regional shopping facilities by the size, number, and variety of their stores.

# Sherway Gardens: A Case Study

## Materials

Copy of Sherway Gardens directory (*Blackline Master 17.1*)
Coloured pencils or pens

1. (a) Identify the four anchor stores in this mall.
   (b) Account for their locations on the plan.
2. Suggest how the smaller stores in the mall and the anchors complement each other.
3. (a) Comment on the shape and traffic flow in this mall.
   (b) What are the advantages of this pattern?
   (c) What are the disadvantages?
4. (a) Using a different colour of pencil or pen to represent each of the following classifications, construct a "land use" map of Sherway Gardens:
   - books, stationery, and office supplies
   - cameras
   - children's wear
   - jewellery, gift, and specialty shops
   - ladies' fashions
   - men's fashions
   - unisex fashions or shops listed under both ladies' and men's fashions
   - shoe stores
   - home furnishings and decorating
   - services and banks and financial institutions
   - electronics, records, and music
   - restaurants and eateries
   - all other uses
   (b) Describe the pattern that emerges.
   (c) Choose one category of shop and comment on the distribution of this type of shop throughout the mall. The following are some points to consider:
   - Is the distribution an even one throughout the mall?
   - Does clustering occur?

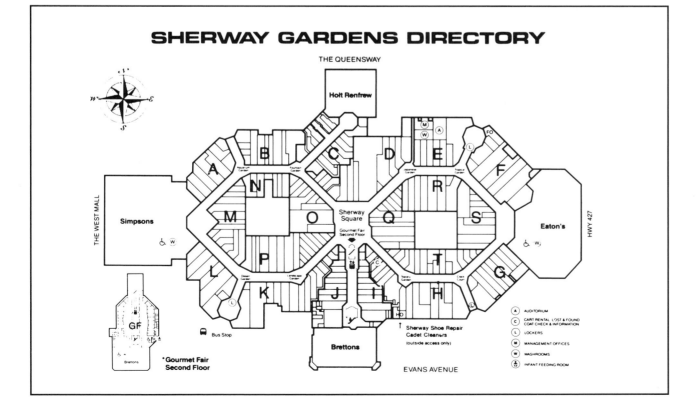

♦ Are all the shops in your category uniformly accessible? Is there one preferred entrance to the mall?

♦ Does the distribution of shops encourage a flow of traffic from one to another?

5. Make up an imaginary multipoint shopping trip with a variety of stops, for example, a bookstore, a department store, a music store, a place for lunch, and unisex fashions. Plan your route through the mall and illustrate your route on the map with arrows.

(a) Does the physical layout of the mall make your trip easier?

(b) What problems, if any, do you encounter?

6. Suggest ways in which the layout and traffic flow of Sherway Gardens could be improved.

# Designing a Shopping Mall

1. Design a shopping mall similar in size and scope to Sherway Gardens. Choose the floor plan that you feel is best suited to the purpose. If a multistorey design is selected, all floors must be shown.

2. Once everyone's designs are finished, they should be displayed and presented to the class for discussion.

## Assessing a Local Shopping Mall

1. Create an inventory of your neighbourhood, community, and regional shopping malls, indicating the size, number, and variety of their stores.

2. What factors or stores might improve a shopping centre that is experiencing poor consumer turnout?

3. Conversely, what impact might the removal of an anchor store have on the success of a shopping centre?

4. What other stores would seriously affect the success of a shopping centre if they were removed?

## Further Study

1. Create a consumer survey to assess what shoppers at a local mall buy when they shop there. Compare results with others in your class.

# Do We Need Another School?

**18**

The planning of schools and their distribution is of paramount importance in urban places. Aside from the obvious social benefits inherent in a well-organized school system, and the massive number of tax dollars absorbed in its maintenance, there are human and spatial considerations that must be taken into account.

Children attending elementary schools tend to have limited mobility. Traditionally, many, if not most, students walk to school. Schools need to be located within comfortable walking distances of the children's homes. This means that, compared with high schools, elementary schools must be more numerous and closer together. Because of the costs involved in the duplication of facilities and staffing, the planning of the distribution and location of elementary schools must be sensitive to both cost and accessibility considerations.

In this assignment, you will analyse the distribution of the public schools in the area of Cambridge, Ontario, using Reilly's Law of Retail Gravitation.

## Assessing the Need for a School

### Materials

Map of public elementary schools in Cambridge, Ontario (*Blackline Masters 18.1 and 18.2*)
Coloured pens or pencils
Calculator

1. Review Reilly's Law of Retail Gravitation (see page 47). Although this exercise does not involve consumer distribution, the Law of Retail Gravitation is relevant here in that both distance and population are factors examined. School populations in this case replace the factor of community population, and the area that consumers are drawn from is replaced by the catchment area of a school.

2. Use a copy of the school distribution map (BLMs 18.1 and 18.2) and the list of school populations to perform your calculations. For each set of adjacent schools on the map, calculate the location of the boundary between the schools. When calculating the distance between schools, use the straight-line distance. Use the formula provided on page 56 for determining the boundaries of the schools in the Cambridge area.

BLM

18.1

18.2

| Schools in Cambridge, Ontario | | | |
|---|---|---|---|
| **School Name** | **Population** | **Map Number** | **Location** |
| Alison Park Public | 254 | 1 | G5 |
| Avenue Road Public | 437 | 2 | E5 |
| Blair Road Public | 280 | 3 | E4 |
| Cecil Cornwell Public | 251 | 6 | F1 |
| Central Public | 300 | 8 | G4 |
| Chalmers Street Public | 281 | 9 | H4 |
| Dickie Settlement Public | 78 | 11 | D1 |
| Dickson Public | 152 | 12 | G4 |
| Galt Collegiate Institute and Vocational School | 1294 | 13 | F4 |
| Glenview Park Secondary | 1143 | 14 | H4 |
| Highland Public | 470 | 17 | F3 |
| Lincoln Avenue Public | 504 | 20 | G5 |
| Little's Corners Public | 78 | 21 | I7 |
| Manchester Public | 300 | 22 | F5 |
| St. Andrew's Senior Public | 491 | 27 | G3 |
| Southwood Secondary | 1134 | 29 | F2 |
| Stewart Avenue Public | 502 | 30 | H4 |
| Tait Street Public | 455 | 31 | H2 |

## Formula for Determining School Boundaries

Distance of boundary from School A

$$= \frac{\text{Distance between School A and School B}}{1 + \sqrt{\dfrac{\text{number of students at School B}}{\text{number of students at School A}}}}$$

3. Indicate, with a pencil, on the map of the schools in Cambridge, the "cutoff" point between each set of adjacent schools. (Note: No elementary school student should have to cross the Grand River.)

4. When all the distances have been calculated and indicated on the map, complete the catchment areas of each school by drawing in coloured pencil or pen a closed circle to indicate the area from which the school is expected to attract pupils.

5. Use a different colour of pencil or pen to complete a similar analysis for the secondary schools in Cambridge. It is possible for secondary school students to cross the Grand River to attend school.

## Conclusion

1. (a) Are the catchment areas of the elementary schools similar in size? Discuss your findings.
   (b) Does your map suggest that all students do not walk to school?
   (c) What do schools to which students must be bussed have in common? How is the overall pattern affected?
   (d) What impact, if any, does the Grand River have on the pattern you have drawn? Are adjustments required to compensate for the disruption the river causes to traffic flows?

2. Do you feel the distribution of elementary schools is efficient? What changes would you make?

3. (a) Do you feel an additional school (or schools) is needed? Explain.
   (b) If you feel that another school (or schools) is needed, indicate on the map in a third colour where this school (or schools) should be located.

4. Analyse the distribution of high schools in Cambridge. What does the distribution suggest about Cambridge as a community?

5. As a planner or trustee, do you feel another high school is warranted in Cambridge? Explain.

## Further Study

1. Conduct a similar distribution study of the schools in your locality. Prepare a list of recommendations for local planners based on your findings.

2. (a) Whether or not your neighbourhood needs another school has became a political issue in your community. The town planners and local politicians have arranged an open forum for the residents of the town to come and air their views on the matter. Decide on one of the following positions for your point of view and then prepare your facts and arguments in advance of the meeting:
   ◆ a concerned parent with no children of high school age
   ◆ a concerned parent with three children in or about to move into high school
   ◆ a small community developer
   ◆ an elderly person in the community
   ◆ a recently graduated high school student
   ◆ an alderman in the community
   ◆ a small retail business person in the neighbourhood
   ◆ an uninformed person, new to the area
   ◆ a position not considered in this list but of interest to you
   (b) Role play a simulation of the arguments that might be heard at that meeting in your town.

# Designing Transport Routes

Are roads just a necessary evil? Urban centres never seem to be able to keep pace with the demand for more roads. As soon as another route is built, traffic only seems to increase, causing more congestion. In the Roman Empire, it was said all roads led to Rome. Can you imagine the traffic chaos that would result if we planned a road system that way today?

In the activity on page 58 you get the chance to play the role of the transportation commissioner for your region. It is your responsibility to develop a highway network linking six urban centres and the regional airport. As a public servant, it is your duty to find the least expensive and most efficient way of linking these seven locations.

**Figure 19.1 San Mateo, California. Comment on the amount of space required for highway interchanges.**

# Road Systems

## Materials

Base map of region *(Blackline Master 19.1)*
Copy of Commissioner's Report on Inter-urban
Transportation *(Blackline Master 19.2)*

1. Determine the location of your regional airport
   on the base map (BLM 19.1).
2. With a pencil, draw several possible routes before you decide on the most efficient route design. Use the Commissioner's Report on Inter-
   urban Transportation and the Cost Estimates
   to calculate the cost of your plan. Note: Your
   road system cannot cross the military base or
   the cemetery, indicated on the base map.
3. Using the legend provided, complete your final
   drawing on the base map (BLM 19.1).
4. Give your highway system a name and print it
   on the map.

## Conclusion

1. How would you describe the role of the transportation commissioner based on your experience in this activity? In what ways was the role
   more challenging than you expected?

2. Interview the transportation commissioner or
   supervisor in your city or town. Before the interview, prepare a list of questions that will
   help you find out more about the job and its
   responsibilities, as well as the qualifications
   and experience needed to successfully handle
   the job. Find out what kind of situations the
   commissioner has had to deal with in the community.
3. In what ways does the number of transportation networks affect the quality of lives in an
   urban centre? Prepare a flow chart to illustrate
   your ideas.

## Further Study

1. Choose four of your favourite cities from around
   the world, one from each continent. Create a
   chart to compare transportation and communication networks. What do your findings suggest?

# Inner-City Transportation

20

Your urban centre has now grown into a large regional centre, and traffic congestion has become a major problem in the downtown core. Vehicular traffic on the main routes through your town has become intolerable. Many downtown businesses have expressed concern that people are no longer willing to put up with the aggravation involved in driving downtown; they prefer to travel to the suburban shopping malls. The town council has asked you, as Transportation Commissioner, to consider the following suggestions to address the problem. In either case, land will have to be expropriated to make room for the project.

**Suggested Strategies to Relieve Traffic Congestion**

1. The construction of a ring road to relieve the traffic flow through the centre of town, by diverting through traffic around the downtown area. (The Ring Road Option)
2. The construction of an above-ground rapid transit system to service the downtown core. (The Rapid Transit Option)

Figure 20.1 New York City traffic congestion. Justify the number and use of taxicabs in this photograph.

# Traffic Control

## Materials

Base map of urban centre with symbols *(Blackline Master 20.1)*

Base map of Ring Road Option with tally sheet *(Blackline Master 20.2)*

Base map of Rapid Transit Option with tally sheet *(Blackline Master 20.3)*

Choose one of the strategies suggested—either the Ring Road Option or the Rapid Transit Option. Whichever one you choose, you will have to calculate the costs. Both strategy options require the precise use of the transport system layout shown here and of the scale provided.

## The Ring Road Option

1. Make a copy of the ring road pattern (BLM 20.2) using either tracing paper or a sheet of Mylar. The scale drawing of the ring road must fit as closely as possible to the existing street pattern (BLM 20.1). By manipulating the ring pattern, you will be able to match it to the current road network. You can rotate the ring pattern to any angle, but its size cannot be altered.

2. Once you have determined the precise location, calculate the total cost of land expropriation by tallying all the values of the buildings that currently occupy the proposed ring route. Also expropriate enough land to provide three parking lots (three city lots) adjacent to the entrance and outside the ring road. Use the scale drawings of parking lots for this purpose. Fill in a copy of the Ring Road Cost Tally Sheet (BLM 20.2) to summarize your expropriation costs.

3. Give two reasons why you think the ring road is a better alternative than the rapid transit option.

**Figure 20.2 Ring Road Concept as illustrated by Scarborough Town Centre's perimeter road. Note the elevated rapid transit line which bisects the site.**

## The Rapid Transit Option

1. Make a copy of the rapid transit system pattern (BLM 20.3), using either tracing paper or a sheet of Mylar. Position the traced pattern over the base map (BLM 20.1), choosing a location that interferes as little as possible with the existing road system. The rapid transit lines must, for the most part, occupy space other than existing road space.
2. Once you have determined the precise location of your rapid transit system, calculate the total cost of land expropriation by tallying all the values of the buildings that occupy the space required for your rapid transit route. Further expropriation is to be made to provide three parking lot locations beside any three transit stations. Use the scale drawings of parking lots for this purpose. Fill in a copy of the Cost Tally Sheet to summarize your expropriation costs (BLM 20.3).
3. Give two reasons why you think the rapid transit option is a better alternative than the ring road option.

## Conclusion

1. Compare the number of persons who chose the ring road option with the number who selected the rapid transit system. Suggest three reasons why one option was more popular than the other.
2. The area within the ring road will become more accessible and therefore more in demand. What will happen to land values? Which land uses may be forced out of the central area because of this?

3. Will the construction of the rapid transit system have the same effect on the central core? Why/Why not?
4. What can cities do to discourage people from driving their cars into the downtown areas?
5. Design a poster to promote your transportation design for the inner city.

## Further Study

1. If you were considering opening a commercial venture in your urban centre, what type of store would you open? Where would you locate it and why?
2. Consider a design for either a ring road or rapid transit system for your own community. Which would be more appropriate? Where would you have the system constructed?
3. Survey a sample of your school population to discover what the awareness level is about urban transport pollution. Create opportunities in your survey for your respondents to identify themselves in some way by age, sex, whether they are drivers or not, and so on. Use the statistics collected to support the position that urban transport pollution is a major contributor of pollutants into the atmosphere. Share your findings with your class.
4. In what ways do transportation and communication networks affect the shape and the function of urban centres? Use a local transportation/communication system as a basis for your comments. In addition, see if there are any archival photographs or illustrations of the system to further support this.

# Using Census Information —Choropleth Profile of a City

# 21

Although the structural patterns of an urban place are partly spontaneous in their formation, urban space does tend to follow certain organization principles. Particular kinds of activities seek particular kinds of locations within urban places. With a careful examination of social and economic land use maps, consistent patterns can be discovered on the urban landscape. Several well-known models have been developed in this century in an attempt to identify these patterns.

## The Concentric Zone Model

In this classic model, developed in the mid 1930s by E. Burgess, a member of the Chicago School of urban sociologists, the city is seen as a pattern of five concentric rings growing outward from the city centre (see Figure 21.1). Burgess's model stressed the dynamic nature of the city in that each ring continues to grow and displace the land use in the next zone.

One consideration to bear in mind when examining the concentric zone model is that the Chicago School of urban sociologists tended to regard relative location in terms of time as well as distance (see page 43). Urban land use patterns cannot be expected to conform perfectly with the ideal concentric pattern when such ecological considerations are made.

Because of socio-economic changes since the thirties, the concentric zone model has limited applications in contemporary urban land use patterns.

## The Sector Model

The sector model was developed in 1939 by Homer Hoyt, an economist with the Federal Housing Authority in the United States (see Figure 21.2). Hoyt was attempting to determine the socio-economic patterns in American cities based on an inventory of housing. The information on housing values and conditions was gathered for city blocks and was converted to choropleth maps. In an attempt to summarize all of the information that

**Figure 21.1 The concentric zone theory. 1: CBD; 2: Transition zone; 3: Zone of independent workers' homes; 4: Zone of better residences; 5: Commuter zone.**

**Figure 21.2 The sector theory. Land uses develop around the CBD and expand outward in pie-shaped wedges or sectors. 1: CBD; 2: Wholesale light manufacturing; 3: Low-income residential; 4: Middle-income residential; 5: High-income residential.**

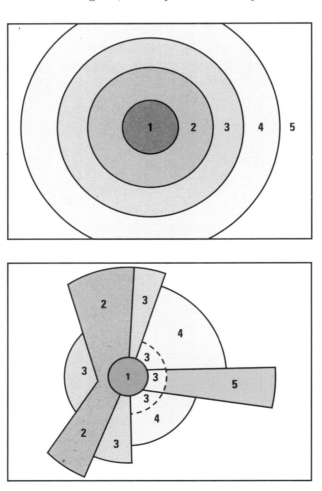

**Figure 21.3**

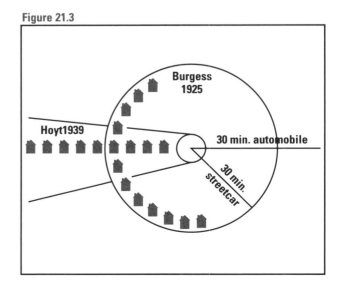

he was able to gather, Hoyt decided to use real property tax as the basis of his theory.

As shown in Figure 21.3, the resulting sector model was more a reflection of how the increased use of the automobile had extended the mobility of the American people. It is interesting to note that, when Hoyt studied the city of Chicago using his criteria, he discovered that the sector pattern emerged.

## The Multiple Nuclei Model

This model was developed by two geographers in 1945. C. Harris and E. Ullman rejected the simple geometric patterns of Burgess and Hoyt as being too inflexible. They felt that the patterns in an urban place were the result of many more factors than could be explained by a single fixed universal model. In looking at a typical land use map of a city, Harris and Ullman believed that the city consisted of a number of decision-making zones, or nuclei, for example, central business district, zoned industrial areas, and various types of residential developments (see Figure 21.4). They thought that each land use evolved from these nuclei and that each city developed differently with respect to these growth points.

**Figure 21.4 The multiple nuclei theory. 1: CBD; 2: Wholesale light manufacturing; 3: Low-income residential; 4: Middle-income residential; 5: High-income residential; 6: Heavy manufacturing; 7: Outlying business district; 8: Residential suburb; 9: Industrial suburb.**

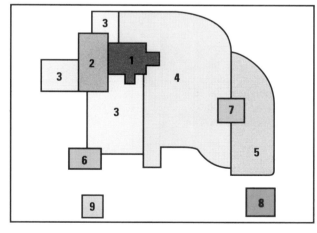

Harris and Ullman have been criticized for failing to stress the unity of the urban place. Their concentration on the details of the urban pattern has been likened to "not seeing the forest for the trees."

It is obvious from this brief summary of the most popular land use pattern models that the urban place is far too complex a phenomenon to be adequately described by a single model. Instead, several models or combinations of models must be used to do justice to the urban landscape. R.A. Murdie's (1969) celebrated study of patterns in Toronto discovered that various characteristics such as ethnic affiliation, socio-economic grouping, and family status groups conformed to patterns that had been discovered in previous studies of other North American cities. Murdie's findings are shown in Figure 21.5.

Murdie identified a pattern of "concentric zones distorted by the underlying pattern of trans-

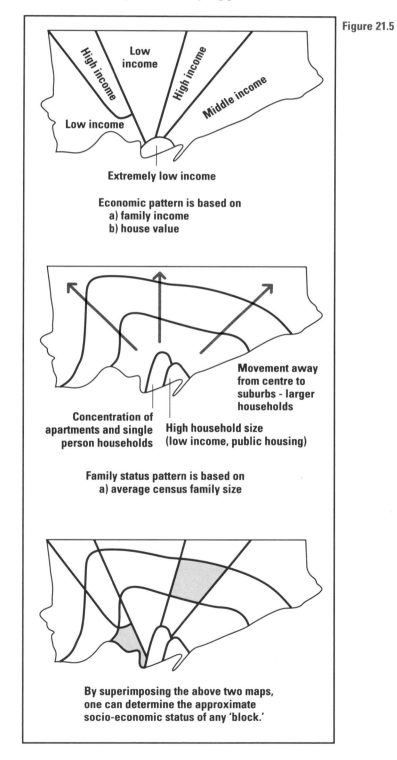

**Figure 21.5**

portation, with small families close to the centre of the city and large families at the periphery."

"Juxtaposed with this concentric pattern is a zonal arrangement of census tracts of low and high economic status families and individuals. Finally, clustered around the Metropolitan area but conforming to the underlying concentric family status and zonal economic patterns are certain ethnic groups."[1]

It can be seen that Burgess's concentric zone model is the basis of family status patterns in urban places. Socio-economic patterns conform to Hoyt's sector model. Ethnic and cultural groups tend to be found in pockets within the urban fabric, as in the multinuclei model of Harris and Ullman. In this assignment, you can investigate this phenomenon using census data and choropleth mapping techniques.

# Presenting the Census Data

## Materials

Base map of Metropolitan Winnipeg (Blackline Master 21.1)
Coloured pencils or pens
In this part of the assignment you are required to construct a choropleth map of Metropolitan Winnipeg. The map is based on information gathered in the 1981 census.

1. On a copy of the census tract map of the greater Winnipeg area (BLM 21.1), construct a choropleth map showing one of the following topics:

   ♦ percentage of population of British origin
   ♦ percentage of population of French origin
   ♦ percentage of population of Ukrainian origin
   ♦ percentage of population of German origin
   ♦ percentage of population of Polish origin
   ♦ percentage of population of Filipino origin
   ♦ percentage of population of Jewish origin
   ♦ percentage of population who are immigrants
   ♦ percentage of population with a university education
   ♦ average family size
   ♦ average house value
   ♦ average family income

2. Each topic is to be displayed on a separate copy of the base map (BLM 21.1). You are to complete at least one choropleth map each.

   In constructing your choropleth maps, the following colour legend *must* be used to keep the maps uniform for comparison purposes:

   | yellow | low values (less than) |
   |--------|------------------------|
   | orange | |
   | red | |
   | blue | |
   | brown | high values (more than) |

3. When arranging the census data for your choropleth maps, use the following classifications:

| | |
|---|---|
| **Av. # of Persons per Census Family** | less than 2.5<br>2.6 - 2.8<br>2.9 - 3.1<br>3.2 - 3.4<br>more than 3.4 |
| **Ethnic Origins** | less than 5%<br>5 - 10%<br>10 - 20%<br>20 - 30%<br>more than 30% |
| **Total Immigrant Population** | less than 5%<br>5 - 10%<br>10 - 25%<br>25 - 40%<br>more than 40% |
| **Population over 15 Years of Age with a University Education** | 0 - 6%<br>6 - 14%<br>14 - 20%<br>20 - 28%<br>more than 28% |
| **Average House Value** | less than $45 000<br>$45 000 - $65 000<br>$65 000 - $85 000<br>$85 000 - $105 000<br>more than $105 000 |
| **Average Family Income** | less than $25 000<br>$25 000 - $35 000<br>$35 000 - $45 000<br>$45 000 - $55 000<br>over $55 000 |

[1]Barry Garner and Maurice Yates. THE NORTH AMERICAN CITY. (New York: Harper and Row, 1976)

# Analysing the Patterns

After all the maps have been completed, they should be displayed and analysed.

1. Identify the major patterns on each of the maps. Try to determine if the pattern is concentric, sector, or multinuclei. The patterns may not be obvious at first glance. They are rarely perfect in form, and some imagination may be required to detect a pattern.
2. Are there clearly defined edges to the pattern, such as, rivers or main roads? Does the presence of the Red and Assiniboine rivers seem to have any impact on average house values?

3. How does the pattern on each map relate to the patterns found on the other maps? For example, is there a correlation between average house value and education level?
4. Do the patterns discovered conform with the theories of Burgess, Hoyt, and Harris and Ullman? Discuss your findings.
5. Do the patterns discovered conform with Murdie's observations? Discuss.

## Further Study

1. Investigate the use of computers in compiling and analysing census information further.

**Census Data for Metropolitan Winnipeg (1981)**

| Census Tract No. | Percentage of Population | | | | | | | | | Average | | |
| | British | French | Ukranian | German | Polish | Filipino | Jewish Origin | Total Immigrants | With University Degree | Family Size | House Value $ | Family Income $ |
|---|---|---|---|---|---|---|---|---|---|---|---|---|
| 001 | 26.6 | 1.9 | 2.7 | 5.5 | 1.9 | 1.6 | .4 | 13.3 | 17 | 2.9 | 70 656 | 39 395 |
| 002 | 27.2 | 4.0 | 4.7 | 5.7 | 1.4 | 1.4 | .4 | 15.8 | 9.6 | 3.0 | 49 603 | 30 242 |
| 003 | 22.7 | 3.8 | 7.9 | 5.2 | 1.8 | .9 | 1.3 | 13.9 | 11.4 | 2.8 | 49 317 | 29 600 |
| 004.01 | 22.6 | 2.3 | 6.8 | 6.0 | 2.5 | .1 | 6.5 | 19.0 | 13.2 | 2.7 | 66 604 | 35 887 |
| 004.02 | 21.4 | 3.4 | 5.7 | 5.5 | 3.1 | .1 | 4.2 | 16.7 | 11.1 | 2.6 | 62 911 | 32 695 |
| 005 | 16.6 | 1.3 | 2.3 | 3.2 | .7 | — | 34 | 15.8 | 29.4 | 3.1 | 106 253 | 58 663 |
| 006 | 27.2 | 5 | 4.4 | 5.5 | 1.1 | .3 | 7.5 | 15.6 | 15.3 | 2.8 | 74 264 | 41 441 |
| 007 | 28 | 2.8 | 3.1 | 4.6 | 1.3 | .2 | 1.3 | 14.7 | 20.3 | 2.9 | 74 867 | 39 301 |
| 008 | 25.3 | 1.6 | 2.0 | 8.2 | .6 | — | 7.4 | 15.7 | 37.7 | 3.2 | 120 885 | 64 993 |
| 009 | 30.1 | 1.5 | 1.9 | 2.2 | 1.8 | .5 | 7.1 | 11.5 | 39.2 | 3.1 | 91 513 | 54 118 |
| 010 | 27.4 | 2.6 | 1.9 | 4.3 | 1.3 | .3 | 8.9 | 16.5 | 35.9 | 3.0 | 113 488 | 64 437 |
| 011 | 23.2 | 3.8 | 5.3 | 4.8 | 1.9 | .1 | 12.1 | 18.9 | 28.6 | 2.3 | 78 234 | 44 375 |
| 012 | 18.9 | 5.1 | 3.8 | 5.3 | 1.7 | 1.7 | 3.5 | 22.4 | 16.3 | 2.4 | 61 733 | 22 854 |
| 013 | 23.2 | 3.7 | 6.1 | 5.5 | 1.5 | 2.7 | 3.7 | 24.4 | 12.5 | 2.1 | 60 000 | 26 232 |
| 014 | 20.4 | 4.5 | 6.2 | 7.2 | 3.1 | 1.2 | 2.0 | 23.1 | 15.6 | 2.3 | 60 000 | 24 912 |
| 015 | 23 | 2.7 | 4.4 | 6.0 | 2.8 | 2.9 | 1.4 | 24.1 | 13.6 | 2.6 | 97 195 | 25 687 |
| 016 | 14 | 3.8 | 5.3 | 8.3 | 3.4 | 1.5 | .8 | 23.5 | 17.0 | 2.8 | 62 068 | 30 397 |
| 017 | 16.7 | 3.6 | 5.1 | 8.4 | 1.1 | 1.6 | 1.2 | 21.5 | 25.3 | 2.9 | 69 085 | 34 618 |
| 018 | 22.2 | 2.0 | 6.6 | 10.8 | .4 | .2 | .4 | 19.0 | 14.8 | 2.9 | 69 610 | 37 089 |
| 019 | 24.4 | 1.5 | 5.5 | 10.4 | 1.8 | 5.9 | .3 | 21.7 | 7.2 | 2.9 | 53 064 | 31 754 |
| 020 | 21.4 | 4.4 | 2.9 | 5.6 | 1.6 | 4.8 | .4 | 15.1 | 8.6 | 2.9 | 52 694 | 32 869 |
| 021 | 13.8 | 3.1 | 4.5 | 4.7 | .9 | 11.5 | — | 37.5 | 5.0 | 3.1 | 46 359 | 24 778 |
| 022 | 10.1 | 2.3 | 4.3 | 2.9 | 1.1 | 13.3 | .4 | 42.4 | 3.4 | 3.1 | 43 460 | 17 929 |
| 023 | 16.3 | 2.5 | 4.5 | 2.8 | 2.9 | 10.7 | 1.1 | 37.8 | 6.7 | 2.7 | 34 188 | 17 204 |
| 024 | 10.5 | 4.4 | 10.5 | 3.5 | 6.1 | — | — | 15.8 | 2.0 | 3.0 | 34 804 | 31 239 |
| 025 | 15.2 | 4.0 | 3.0 | .9 | 1.4 | 13.2 | .3 | 45.8 | 3.7 | 3.4 | 55 156 | 15 515 |
| 026 | 13.0 | 3.4 | 4.9 | 2.6 | 1.7 | 17.6 | — | 47.2 | 5.2 | 3.3 | 49 097 | 20 060 |
| 027 | 13.7 | 2.2 | 4.2 | 7.0 | 1.1 | 9.8 | — | 35.0 | 9.8 | 3.1 | 52 269 | 24 851 |
| 028 | 10.5 | 1.6 | 2.7 | 4.2 | 1.2 | 17.2 | .2 | 50.0 | 5.4 | 3.2 | 42 574 | 21 487 |
| 029 | 15.2 | 2.0 | 1.6 | 10.8 | 1.2 | 14.9 | — | 43.9 | 5.4 | 3.2 | 47 292 | 25 022 |
| 030 | 21.0 | 1.5 | 4.4 | 7.3 | 1.5 | 12.8 | — | 33.1 | 5.2 | 3.0 | 51 913 | 32 988 |
| 031 | 21.9 | 1.9 | 6.1 | 11.9 | 2.6 | 2.8 | — | 24.4 | 6.7 | 2.8 | 57 650 | 31 422 |
| 032 | 25.2 | 2.8 | 6.2 | 5.6 | 1.9 | 5.1 | .2 | 15.4 | 1.4 | 3.0 | 41 620 | 25 781 |
| 033 | 12.9 | 1.9 | 6.7 | 2.4 | 1.9 | — | — | 39.7 | — | 3.3 | 37 924 | 22 973 |
| 034 | 11.6 | 3.7 | 11.2 | 1.2 | 13.9 | 5.2 | .2 | 29.4 | 3.3 | 3.3 | 48 037 | 17 572 |
| 035 | 12.7 | 1.7 | 15.9 | 1.5 | 5.8 | 2.6 | — | 19.5 | 4.8 | 3.1 | 44 004 | 21 512 |

| Census Tract No. | Percentage of Population | | | | | | | | | Average | | |
|---|---|---|---|---|---|---|---|---|---|---|---|---|
| | British | French | Ukranian | German | Polish | Filipino | Jewish Origin | Total Immigrants | With University Degree | Family Size | House Value $ | Family Income $ |
| 036 | 10.5 | 4.7 | 16.8 | 2.0 | 6.3 | 5.8 | — | 15.7 | 2.1 | 3.0 | 38 143 | 20 557 |
| 037 | 19.8 | 5.7 | 14.1 | 14.4 | 3.4 | 1.6 | .3 | 17.8 | 4.0 | 2.9 | 62 088 | 31 452 |
| 038 | 24.2 | 3.8 | 9.1 | 8.6 | 3.4 | .7 | .2 | 16.1 | 3.9 | 2.9 | 46 563 | 25 594 |
| 039 | 22.7 | 3.8 | 8.6 | 9.4 | 1.9 | 2.2 | — | 19.7 | 3.8 | 2.9 | 44 150 | 25 244 |
| 040 | 17.8 | 3.3 | 6.0 | 11.0 | 5.5 | 1.8 | .9 | 16.7 | 12.2 | 3.1 | 56 124 | 32 311 |
| 041 | 13.4 | 2.5 | 13.5 | 6.8 | 4.7 | 2.8 | 7.3 | 20.4 | 10.0 | 3.1 | 58 515 | 32 711 |
| 042 | 9.8 | 3.3 | 11.7 | 4.8 | 4.8 | 11.6 | 1.7 | 29.4 | 4.0 | 3.1 | 42 424 | 22 224 |
| 043 | 12.8 | 3.5 | 18.7 | 3.8 | 7.0 | 11.2 | .3 | 27.6 | 1.7 | 3.1 | 37 981 | 20 707 |
| 044 | 16.4 | 4.8 | 19.0 | 5.0 | 6.5 | 6.7 | — | 18.7 | 4.3 | 3.0 | 36 927 | 23 349 |
| 045 | 12.0 | 2.4 | 14.3 | 6.2 | 7.2 | 14.1 | .5 | 27.7 | 3.7 | 3.1 | 42 257 | 24 738 |
| 046 | 13.9 | 3.5 | 10.6 | 3.3 | 6.8 | 4.7 | 6.1 | 26.6 | 6.0 | 2.9 | 51 810 | 25 414 |
| 047 | 14.0 | 2.2 | 20.3 | 8.2 | 7.8 | 3.8 | 6.8 | 24.2 | 6.5 | 2.9 | 49 658 | 29 290 |
| 048 | 14.7 | 2.7 | 23.9 | 6.2 | 5.1 | 5.2 | .6 | 19.9 | 2.6 | 2.8 | 45 667 | 29 184 |
| 049 | 13.3 | 1.2 | 30.6 | 10.8 | 7.3 | 1.0 | .6 | 21.0 | 2.6 | 2.7 | 61 572 | 32 582 |
| 050.01 | 24.0 | 2.7 | 6.5 | 3.6 | 3.6 | 2.1 | .5 | 9.1 | 2.6 | 3.2 | 48 254 | 24 118 |
| 050.02 | 17.5 | 3.0 | 18.3 | 6.9 | 10.1 | 1.1 | .3 | 23 | 2.1 | 2.9 | 57 953 | 32 643 |
| 051.01 | 13.4 | 1.7 | 6.9 | 4.4 | 1.9 | 13.7 | .5 | 28.5 | 5.6 | 3.4 | 71 263 | 34 868 |
| 051.02 | 17.2 | 3.2 | 6.9 | 4.0 | 1.3 | 10.9 | .4 | 23.0 | 8.4 | 3.5 | 79 093 | 37 390 |
| 052 | — | — | — | — | — | — | — | — | — | — | — | — |
| 100.01 | 19.6 | 9.4 | 4.5 | 5.8 | .8 | 2.0 | .1 | 12.5 | 14.0 | 3.1 | 84 690 | 40 891 |
| 100.02 | 10.5 | 10.5 | 7.0 | 9.6 | 1.3 | — | — | 11.4 | 14.4 | 3.5 | 140 777 | 53 442 |
| 101.01 | 23.1 | 6.7 | 5.5 | 8.3 | 1.1 | .1 | .6 | 11.2 | 16.6 | 3.1 | 94 336 | 52 055 |
| 101.02 | 17.3 | 7.6 | 6.0 | 6.2 | 1.0 | 2.3 | — | 12.8 | 14.4 | 3.4 | 99 325 | 45 224 |
| 102.01 | 18.7 | 12.8 | 4.1 | 8.4 | 1.0 | .7 | .1 | 12.8 | 9.2 | 3.4 | 79 971 | 39 675 |
| 102.02 | 22.4 | 13.3 | 6.0 | 5.4 | 1.5 | — | .5 | 10.7 | 8.6 | 2.8 | 63 901 | 30 580 |
| 102.03 | 26.0 | 10.8 | 6.8 | 7.4 | 1.3 | .5 | .3 | 11.9 | 3.8 | 2.8 | 67 929 | 31 644 |
| 102.04 | 22.1 | 12.0 | 5.3 | 7.4 | 1.7 | .4 | .2 | 11.2 | 9.7 | 2.8 | 63 934 | 24 441 |
| 103 | 28.3 | 5.4 | 3.7 | 3.7 | 2.2 | .2 | .3 | 8.7 | 22.5 | 2.9 | 88 289 | 46 869 |
| 104 | 35.0 | 12.4 | 5.6 | 5.7 | 1.6 | — | .3 | 13.5 | 5.8 | 2.6 | 55 356 | 31 862 |
| 105 | 22.5 | 18.5 | 3.9 | 6.1 | 1.1 | — | .2 | 11.3 | 6.1 | 2.8 | 56 156 | 34 738 |
| 110.01 | 18.7 | 35.2 | 2.2 | 3.3 | — | — | — | 6.6 | 0 | 3.3 | 69 099 | 35 451 |
| 110.02 | 22.5 | 10.2 | 5.0 | 5.7 | 1.6 | .1 | — | 14.1 | 19.4 | 3.5 | 109 248 | 58 902 |
| 110.03 | 16.2 | 11.7 | 6.9 | 6.7 | 1.0 | 2.5 | — | 17.1 | 22.1 | 3.4 | 124 970 | 50 581 |
| 111 | 21.4 | 18.4 | 5.8 | 5.0 | 1.3 | .1 | .2 | 10.0 | 9.1 | 3.3 | 79 458 | 45 911 |
| 112.01 | 15.2 | 19.7 | 6.8 | 4.9 | 1.5 | .8 | — | 13.6 | 7.6 | 3.2 | 70 499 | 40 306 |
| 112.02 | 20.5 | 18.0 | 6.2 | 3.8 | 1.2 | .5 | .4 | 10.6 | 8.8 | 3.1 | 66 905 | 37 446 |
| 113 | 13.6 | 25.6 | 7.2 | 3.8 | 2.8 | — | — | 11.5 | 4.1 | 2.9 | 57 267 | 31 369 |
| 114 | 16.3 | 37.4 | 4.1 | 2.9 | .6 | .4 | — | 11.7 | 9.8 | 2.9 | 60 409 | 33 616 |
| 115 | 21.5 | 17.5 | 4.5 | 2.9 | 1.7 | .8 | — | 9.4 | 19.4 | 3.0 | 73 461 | 43 499 |
| 116 | 8.9 | 47.4 | 2.3 | 2.4 | 1.4 | .2 | .2 | 9.4 | 9.7 | 2.7 | 61 005 | 28 922 |
| 117 | 5.5 | 53.9 | 1.2 | 1.5 | .5 | — | — | 6.2 | 9.1 | 3.0 | 56 534 | 32 873 |
| 120.01 | 21.5 | 6.8 | 9.3 | 6.2 | 2.4 | 3.4 | — | 12.5 | 3.3 | 3.5 | 67 146 | 36 158 |
| 120.02 | 18.8 | 3.2 | 6.7 | 7.3 | 2.8 | .3 | — | 12.7 | 8.9 | 3.5 | 63 482 | 36 107 |
| 120.03 | 22.9 | 2.8 | 7.9 | 9.4 | 2.3 | — | .1 | 10.9 | 3.9 | 3.4 | 68 696 | 38 678 |
| 121 | 27.3 | 3.6 | 15.2 | 9.0 | 4.2 | — | — | 9.0 | 5.2 | 3.1 | 66 103 | 41 844 |
| 122 | 20.9 | 2.9 | 12.1 | 6.0 | 2.3 | .5 | .1 | 10.0 | 5.5 | 3.2 | 64 622 | 38 005 |
| 123 | 19.8 | 5.1 | 13.0 | 5.8 | 2.3 | .3 | .2 | 10.4 | 4.4 | 3.2 | 59 414 | 37 756 |
| 130.01 | 23.3 | 2.0 | 13.5 | 10.9 | 2.9 | .6 | — | 16.0 | 5.9 | 3.0 | 64 252 | 34 476 |
| 130.02 | 19.1 | 4.4 | 8.5 | 9.6 | 2.1 | 1.3 | .2 | 13.1 | 5.2 | 3.2 | 65 581 | 31 758 |
| 131 | 19.1 | 3.8 | 14.0 | 9.1 | 4.6 | .8 | .2 | 19.3 | 4.2 | 2.8 | 49 735 | 34 740 |
| 132 | 21.6 | 1.6 | 15.4 | 13.1 | 4.2 | — | — | 14.5 | 13.7 | 2.8 | 88 939 | 42 978 |
| 133 | 23.3 | 1.7 | 16.0 | 10.2 | 3.4 | 2.2 | — | 16.3 | 13.8 | 2.8 | 60 429 | 33 439 |
| 134 | 18.9 | 2.3 | 15.8 | 13.5 | 3.7 | .6 | — | 17.9 | 7.1 | 2.9 | 73 083 | 38 733 |
| 140.01 | 13.2 | 2.8 | 9.5 | 11.7 | 2.9 | 1.1 | .1 | 16.8 | 5.8 | 3.5 | 80 981 | 39 845 |
| 140.02 | 18.4 | 2.7 | 8.0 | 12.0 | 2.3 | — | .1 | 10.5 | 10.1 | 3.3 | 91 516 | 43 497 |
| 140.03 | 12.2 | 2.9 | 12.8 | 11.1 | 2.3 | — | — | 16.9 | 7.6 | 3.5 | 106 670 | 51 235 |
| 141.01 | 18.4 | 2.1 | 9.5 | 27.0 | 2.7 | .1 | — | 20.3 | 7.6 | 3.0 | 78 101 | 40 639 |

| Census Tract No. | Percentage of Population | | | | | | | | | Average | | |
|---|---|---|---|---|---|---|---|---|---|---|---|---|
| | British | French | Ukranian | German | Polish | Filipino | Jewish Origin | Total Immigrants | With University Degree | Family Size | House Value $ | Family Income $ |
| 141.02 | 12.7 | 1.4 | 7.5 | 33.1 | 4.6 | — | .7 | 30.9 | 8.4 | 2.9 | 74 057 | 34 080 |
| 142.01 | 17.3 | 2.8 | 8.7 | 21.1 | 2.5 | .9 | — | 17.4 | 8.7 | 3.2 | 91 562 | 37 194 |
| 142.02 | 14.1 | 2.0 | 12.7 | 17.3 | 3.1 | .6 | — | 14.8 | 15.9 | 3.5 | 115 083 | 50 836 |
| 142.03 | 24.7 | 2.5 | 10.1 | 16.5 | 3.1 | .1 | .4 | 19.5 | 9.8 | 2.4 | 112 071 | 39 740 |
| 142.04 | 15.2 | 3.6 | 10.3 | 17.7 | 1.7 | .5 | .2 | 18.6 | 5.9 | 3.4 | 78 723 | 37 341 |
| 150 | 17.3 | 2.3 | 12.9 | 12.9 | 4.0 | — | 1.4 | 11.4 | 10.8 | 3.4 | 127 666 | 48 741 |
| 500.01 | 23.1 | 3.0 | 5.8 | 8.7 | 2.2 | .8 | .4 | 19.5 | 25.6 | 3.2 | 96 520 | 44 662 |
| 500.02 | 18.8 | 15.2 | 2.0 | 4.4 | .6 | 1.1 | .4 | 14.1 | 12.5 | 3.3 | 77 220 | 42 901 |
| 500.03 | 21.9 | 5.6 | 4.4 | 5.8 | .2 | 1.6 | — | 16.8 | 23.7 | 3.4 | 108 329 | 49 832 |
| 500.04 | 21.3 | 3.9 | 5.4 | 5.6 | 1.3 | .1 | .7 | 19.2 | 24.4 | 3.3 | 103 910 | 44 557 |
| 501.01 | 21.8 | 3.8 | 4.9 | 8.9 | 2.4 | .1 | .4 | 16.3 | 21.0 | 2.6 | 86 404 | 37 322 |
| 501.02 | 19.4 | 4.0 | 4.9 | 5.5 | .9 | .8 | .3 | 20.2 | 16.5 | 3.3 | 84 094 | 42 252 |
| 502 | 22.8 | 2.0 | 6.9 | 11.2 | 1.6 | — | — | 12.6 | 10.2 | 3.0 | 66 843 | 37 405 |
| 503 | 31 | .9 | 3.8 | 5.3 | .8 | .7 | 1.2 | 16.3 | 25.2 | 3.0 | 90 087 | 54 237 |
| 510 | 18.5 | 1.3 | 3.0 | 4.7 | .6 | 3.4 | 18.8 | 21.4 | 32.6 | 3.2 | 199 771 | 93 971 |
| 520.01 | 24.1 | 1.2 | 5.3 | 8.6 | .8 | .8 | — | 15.1 | 11.2 | 3.4 | 119 973 | 46 237 |
| 520.02 | 20.2 | 2.0 | 3.3 | 9.1 | 1.8 | — | — | 12.4 | 22.4 | 3.6 | 145 381 | 65 340 |
| 520.03 | 21.9 | 2.8 | 5.4 | 6.8 | 1.3 | — | .2 | 10.2 | 10.9 | 3.4 | 83 880 | 41 793 |
| 521 | 25.0 | 3.0 | 4.1 | 8.7 | 1.4 | — | .6 | 12.0 | 13.4 | 3.3 | 100 034 | 46 686 |
| 522.01 | 25.2 | 3.4 | 3.3 | 7.7 | .8 | — | .3 | 13.0 | 14.6 | 3.0 | 104 485 | 51 408 |
| 522.02 | 25.8 | 3.0 | 4.4 | 5.7 | 1.3 | — | .8 | 13.6 | 20.5 | 3.3 | 114 336 | 55 020 |
| 530 | 33.5 | 5.2 | 3.7 | 4.9 | .3 | — | .3 | 13.3 | 16.5 | 2.8 | 74 259 | 41 703 |
| 531 | 29.9 | 3.4 | 4.2 | 4.9 | 1.1 | 1.4 | .1 | 13.3 | 3.8 | 2.7 | 48 187 | 29 429 |
| 532 | 30.1 | 2.1 | 4.2 | 5.2 | 3.1 | 2.1 | — | 10.9 | 4.7 | 3.0 | 55 530 | 34 374 |
| 533 | 34.6 | 3.4 | 2.7 | 4.8 | 1.0 | .8 | .6 | 12.3 | 11.5 | 2.9 | 71 701 | 40 728 |
| 534 | 33.4 | 2.2 | 3.9 | 5.3 | .3 | .6 | — | 15.5 | 11.9 | 2.7 | 85 783 | 37 828 |
| 535 | 36.2 | 4.6 | 3.8 | 4.3 | 1.6 | — | — | 11.4 | 7.5 | 3.0 | 75 463 | 40 683 |
| 536 | 32.4 | 2.3 | 4.5 | 6.4 | 1.8 | .3 | .3 | 13.6 | 14.9 | 2.9 | 98 009 | 47 224 |
| 537.01 | 34.7 | 2.7 | 4.2 | 8.3 | 1.4 | .3 | — | 15.1 | 11.1 | 3.0 | 105 628 | 48 127 |
| 537.02 | 30.7 | 2.0 | 4.9 | 9.5 | 1.3 | — | .1 | 11.5 | 19.7 | 3.3 | 102 774 | 59 065 |
| 537.03 | 28.1 | 2.0 | 5.9 | 7.0 | 1.0 | — | .1 | 10.9 | 13.3 | 3.2 | 84 819 | 47 005 |
| 538 | 30.8 | 4.9 | 9.2 | 8.6 | .2 | — | — | 10.2 | 12.9 | 3.2 | 82 585 | 48 567 |
| 539.01 | 27.0 | 2.0 | 4.4 | 5.0 | .6 | — | .1 | 12.9 | 7.4 | 3.4 | 77 272 | 38 639 |
| 539.02 | 26.7 | 2.3 | 6.9 | 3.7 | .5 | 1.1 | .1 | 12.4 | 6.2 | 3.3 | 75 864 | 38 477 |
| 540.01 | 28.1 | 2.2 | 5.4 | 7.3 | 1.1 | — | — | 15.4 | 9.0 | 3.5 | 83 000 | 46 239 |
| 540.02 | 29.5 | 5.1 | 4.3 | 8.4 | 1.2 | .6 | — | 10.9 | 5.1 | 3.1 | 77 913 | 39 882 |
| 540.03 | 30.3 | 2.5 | 3.5 | 6.2 | 1.3 | .9 | .2 | 15.8 | 14.0 | 3.0 | 95 640 | 41 341 |
| 540.04 | 23.2 | 2.7 | 7.1 | 8.5 | 1.8 | — | .2 | 11.1 | 7.2 | 3.0 | 81 191 | 38 423 |
| 541 | 46.0 | 14.4 | .9 | 2.7 | — | — | — | 9.0 | 5.7 | 3.2 | — | 33 498 |
| 542 | 28.0 | 4.6 | 9.1 | 4.4 | 1.9 | 1.9 | — | 13.9 | 1.4 | 3.0 | 41 722 | 25 071 |
| 550 | 21.5 | 1.1 | 17.0 | 8.2 | 6.5 | — | 6.7 | 22.6 | 9.8 | 2.8 | 63 703 | 38 771 |
| 551 | 14.4 | 1.9 | 19.7 | 7.1 | 9.3 | .8 | 13.5 | 25.4 | 5.9 | 2.7 | 59 097 | 35 051 |
| 552.01 | 9.4 | 1.0 | 21.3 | 6.3 | 6.3 | 1.4 | 22.5 | 25.7 | 9.5 | 3.0 | 95 568 | 46 286 |
| 552.02 | 6.7 | 1.8 | 14.6 | 3.7 | 5.1 | — | 40.5 | 28.6 | 17.0 | 3.1 | 124 800 | 50 545 |
| 553 | 17.1 | 2.1 | 19.8 | 6.5 | 8.4 | 1.9 | 7.8 | 24.8 | 5.7 | 2.9 | 68 922 | 32 983 |
| 560.01 | 8.6 | 1.7 | 9.7 | 3.4 | 1.7 | 19.0 | 2.6 | 26.4 | 10.0 | 3.4 | 92 205 | 39 796 |
| 560.02 | 13.4 | 2.0 | 9.4 | 5.4 | 3.9 | 9.8 | 6.4 | 27.0 | 6.8 | 3.3 | 79 712 | 34 043 |
| 560.03 | 16.2 | 1.9 | 13.4 | 7.2 | 5.7 | 2.2 | 2.4 | 18.2 | 8.3 | 3.2 | 83 635 | 36 882 |
| 560.04 | 12.2 | 1.7 | 10.7 | 5.6 | 4.4 | 6.9 | 5.7 | 28.7 | 10.4 | 3.4 | 81 441 | 39 732 |
| 570 | 19.0 | 3.0 | 14.0 | 9.3 | 7.3 | — | .2 | 13.6 | 7.9 | 3.3 | 113 546 | 44 997 |
| 580 | 17.5 | 13.3 | 2.4 | 11.5 | .6 | — | — | 13.3 | 4.8 | 3.3 | 106 121 | 36 631 |
| 585 | 23.5 | 1.1 | 5.0 | 16.2 | 2.3 | — | — | 8.9 | 7.4 | 3.2 | 91 741 | 40 096 |
| 590 | 17.6 | 3.6 | 13.0 | 11.2 | 5.1 | — | .2 | 7.8 | 6.1 | 3.3 | 91 065 | 36 791 |
| 595 | 12.9 | 23.8 | 3.1 | 14.9 | .7 | .3 | .1 | 5.7 | 5.9 | 3.7 | 69 687 | 35 947 |
| 600 | 11.8 | 32.7 | 4.4 | 9.7 | 2.2 | — | — | 3.9 | 8.3 | 3.5 | 75 094 | 39 806 |
| WINNIPEG CMA | 20.3 | 5.6 | 7.7 | 7.3 | 2.5 | 2.5 | 2.2 | 17.9 | 11.5 | 3.1 | 77 844 | 38 705 |

# Central Business District Study

The area of most concentrated commercial/service/financial activity in an urban place is referred to as the **central business district (CBD)**. In large metropolitan cities the CBD is easily identified as the cluster of highest buildings on the skyline. In smaller towns and cities, the area and magnitude of the CBD may be considerably reduced. A small town's CBD may consist of a block or two of three-storey commercial buildings surrounded by residential areas.

It is in all CBDs that one finds the greatest concentration of commercial activity and daytime population densities, as well as the **point of maximum accessibility (PMA)** and **peak value intersection (PVI)**. In an area of such concentration, the number of potential business contacts is very high. In addition to face-to-face contact, the CBD facilitates the movement of paper (agreements, receipts, reports, and documents that require signatures and confidential handling), in many cases by bicycle courier.

**Figure 22.1 Calgary Central Business District. The shadows clearly indicate the CBD in this aerial view.**

**Point of Maximum Accessibility (PMA):**
This term refers to the point or intersection in an urban place that is most accessible to the greatest number of people living in the urban place. Typically, the PMA is the same location as the PVI and is a centre of intense financial and commercial activity.

**Peak Value Intersection (PVI):** This term refers to the intersection or point in the central business district with the highest land value. The PVI is usually also the point of minimum aggregate travel costs and effort for the entire urban place.

The clustering of similar financial and retail businesses in close proximity has the benefit of offering relatively easy accessibility to the maximum number of clients with the least amount of effort. Businesses are able to complement one another and to warrant "spinoff" support activities. For example, where there is a large concentration of offices, services such as printing shops, computer consultants, and restaurants will spring up.

A location in the CBD provides a firm with visibility in the business community and the prestige of being able to afford an expensive "downtown" address.

Even in the case of large metropolitan areas, the CBD has a limited horizontal scale rarely exceeding 1.5 km. This clearly illustrates the primacy of pedestrian traffic within the CBD.

Vehicular movement, and even public transit, is hindered by traffic congestion and the lack of parking space. The CBD is best suited to a walking scale. The extended horizontal scale of the CBD, that is, tall buildings served by high-speed express elevators, further demonstrates the importance of pedestrian mobility within the CBD.

Because there are no established standards for fixing the boundaries of the CBD, individual urban places have used a variety of criteria to establish the areas of their CBDs. These include such factors as building height, land value, trade figures, and traffic flows. In many cases, unique local geographical features have been used to help fix the edges of the CBD.

It has been suggested that in the case of metropolitan CBDs a rough "rule of thumb" for visualizing the area of the CBD would be to lay the tallest building in the CBD on its side. Using the height of the building as a compass and tracing a circle provides the approximate area of the CBD. (See Figure 22.2.)

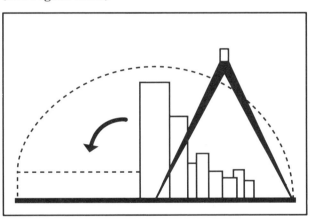

Figure 22.2

# The Murphy And Vance Method of CBD Identification

Although such methods of defining CBD boundaries do serve a purpose, it is obvious that for comparative studies, a standardized method that can be applied to any urban place is required. Perhaps the most useful method developed to date is that of R. E. Murphy and J. E. Vance (1954). In the Murphy and Vance method, the city block is the base area used. After an initial classification of land uses into CBD and non-CBD, two index numbers are calculated for each block. The index numbers are based on information gathered in field observations and other data.

One of the index numbers, the **central business intensity index** (CBII), is used to de-

scribe the percentage of the total floor area in a city block devoted to CBD uses. The higher the value of the CBII, the greater the intensity of the CBD functions in that block.

The second index number, the **central business height index** (CBHI), is concerned with the height of buildings housing CBD activities. As tall buildings are associated with the CBD, the CBHI is used to confirm the CBII findings. Together, the two index numbers are used to determine whether or not a city block is classified as part of the CBD. Outlined below is the Murphy and Vance method of identifying the CBD.

## Procedure for Using the Murphy and Vance Method

### Materials

CBD delimitation field notes form (*Blackline Master 22.1*)
City block maps

### Fieldwork

1. Using a map showing city blocks (and individual buildings if possible), estimate the size of the CBD based on local experience and observation. The study area should be larger than the area tentatively identified as the CBD. (See Figure 22.3.)
2. Each group of students should study one city block. A sketch map should be prepared for each block. (See Figure 22.4.)
3. Each building and lot should be identified by a number on your map. (See Figure 22.5.)
4. In the next step it is necessary to identify which activities in the buildings are CBD and which are non-CBD. Murphy and Vance used an exclusive method to identify CBD land uses. This means that they listed non-CBD uses and classified any activity *not* on this list as a CBD use.

---

#### Noncentral Business District Uses*

Permanent residences (including apartment houses and rooming houses)
Government and public (including parks and public schools, as well as establishments carrying out city, country, provincial, and federal government functions)
Organizational institutions (churches, colleges, fraternal orders, etc.)
Industrial establishments (except for newspapers)
Wholesaling
Vacant buildings and stores
Vacant lots
Commercial storage and warehousing
Railroad tracks and switching yards

*\* All other uses are considered as CBD uses.*

---

5. Use the chart provided (BLM 22.1) to record your data.
6. Each group should appoint a designated "pacer." The length of this person's average stride should be measured.
7. Starting at any corner of the block being examined, pace off the size of each building and note the number of storeys in each building. Record

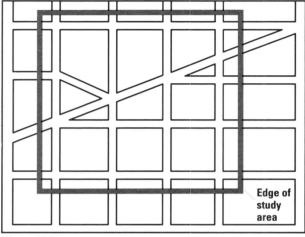

**Figure 22.3**

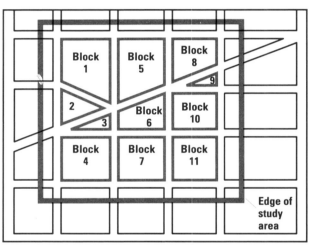

**Figure 22.4**

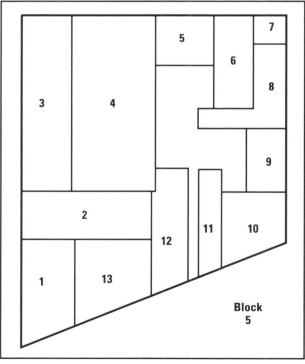

**Figure 22.5**

information on your data sheet (BLM 22.1). In order for the data collected to be consistent, the same person should do the pacing for the group. Striding is not recommended; normal walking is less conspicuous and will produce more accurate results.

## Analysis

Back at school the data collected must be reduced to a CBII index number and a CBHI index number for each block.

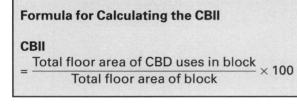

**Formula for Calculating the CBII**

$$CBII = \frac{\text{Total floor area of CBD uses in block}}{\text{Total floor area of block}} \times 100$$

The index number obtained represents the percentage of the total floor area (all storeys of all buildings), devoted to CBD uses.

**Formula for Calculating the CBHI**

$$CBHI = \frac{\text{Total floor area of CBD uses in block}}{\text{Total ground floor area of block}}$$

The index number obtained can be thought of as the number of floors of CBD use that would cover the entire block if these floors were spread evenly over the block. For example, a CBHI of 1.5 would mean that the amount of floor space needed to accommodate the CBD uses on this block would occupy a building of 1.5 storeys covering the entire block.

Based on their observations of many urban places, Murphy and Vance decided that, for a block to be considered part of the CBD, it needed a CBII

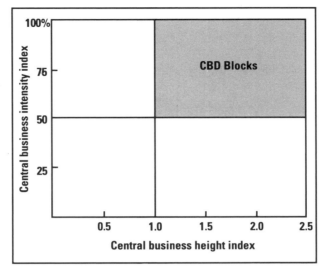

Figure 22.6

of at least 50% *and* a CBHI of at least 1.0. These classifications can be seen in the graph. (See Figure 22.6.) Note that only blocks meeting both CBII and CBHI qualifications are considered part of the CBD.

Because the Murphy and Vance method of defining CBD Boundaries uses index numbers that are the result of a formula and individual city blocks, it can be applied to urban areas of any size.

## Conclusion

1. At this point you are ready to present your findings. Use coloured pens or pencils to indicate the following information on a copy of the map prepared in Step 1 in this activity, page 70.
   (a) the blocks you have identified as belonging to the CBD (dark red);
   (b) the blocks that meet either the CBII or CBHI requirements but not both (light red);
   (c) the rest of the map area (yellow).

# Murvan: A Case Study

## Materials

Base map of the city of Murvan *(Blackline Master 22.2)*
CBD delimitation field notes

1. Using the data given on page 72 for selected blocks in the hypothetical city of Murvan,

complete the calculations needed to arrive at the CBII and CBHI for the specified blocks. The data for Block 20 is presented as a simulation of an actual data sheet prepared on a field trip. The other blocks have the information needed for the Murphy and Vance formula already tabulated.

**CBD DELIMITATION FIELD NOTES**

| DATE:_____ | DATA COMPILED BY:_____ |
|---|---|
| BLOCK NUMBER:_____20_____ | _____ |
| | _____ |
| | _____ |

TOTAL FLOOR AREA OF BLOCK:_____m²
TOTAL GROUND FLOOR AREA OF BLOCK:_____40 000_____m²

| Building Number | Area of Ground Floor | Number of Floors | Area of Non-CBD use | Area of CBD use |
|---|---|---|---|---|
| 1 | 12 500 m² | 10 | 100 000 m² | 25 000 m² |
| 2 | 2 500 m² | 4 | none | 10 000 m² |
| 3 | 2 500 m² | 6 | 2 000 m² | 13 000 m² |
| 4 | 7 500 m² | 3 | none | 22 500 m² |
| 5 | 4 000 m² | 2 | 1 000 m² | 7 000 m² |
| 6 | 4 000 m² | 5 | 18 000 m² | 2 000 m² |
| 7 | 8 750 m² | 6 | 2 500 m² | 50 000 m² |

**DATA FOR SELECTED BLOCKS IN MURVAN**

| Block Number | Total Ground Floor Area of Block | Total Floor Area of CBD Uses in Block | Total Floor Area of Block |
|---|---|---|---|
| 9 | 60 000 m² | 50 000 m² | 105 000 m² |
| 10 | 25 000 m² | 20 000 m² | 40 000 m² |
| 11 | 25 000 m² | 15 000 m² | 55 000 m² |
| 12 | 50 000 m² | 60 000 m² | 150 000 m² |
| 13 | 20 000 m² | 10 000 m² | 30 000 m² |
| 14 | 20 000 m² | 12 000 m² | 32 000 m² |
| 18 | 50 000 m² | 30 000 m² | 95 000 m² |
| 19 | 20 000 m² | 40 000 m² | 50 000 m² |
| 20 | | (see block data above) | |
| 21 | 20 000 m² | 15 000 m² | 55 000 m² |
| 22 | 20 000 m² | 130 000 m² | 140 000 m² |
| 23 | 20 000 m² | 170 000 m² | 175 000 m² |
| 25 | 20 000 m² | 10 000 m² | 45 000 m² |
| 26 | 40 000 m² | 30 000 m² | 90 000 m² |

(a) Complete the calculations needed to arrive at the CBII and CBHI for Block 20.
(b) Complete the calculations needed to arrive at the CBII and CBHI for the other blocks.

2. On a copy of the base map of Murvan (BLM 22.2), indicate the blocks you have identified as the CBD.

(a) Indicate on the map where you think the PVI would be located. How did you reach this decision?
(b) In what direction do you think the CBD of Murvan will move in the future? Give reasons for your answer.

## Further Study

1. With the increasing use of such technologies as extensive computer networks and fax machines, the need for the CBD may be on the decline. Comment on the decentralization of the CBD in the future.
2. The CBD is rarely located at the geographic centre of an urban place. Comment on the location of most CBDs.
3. Using data and maps of your local community, complete a CBD study using the Murphy and Vance method. Along with local area CBD maps, you would also require a copy of the CBD Delimitation Field Notes form (BLM 22.1).

# Not in My Backyard (NIMBY) –Designing an Infill Project

# 23

Well, it's finally happened! You and your neighbours have just had some bad news. The price of land in the city, being as high as it is, has prompted developers to propose a more efficient use of some of the space within your local neighbourhood. A tract of land, the old Cannon Estate, dating back to the 1820s, which is currently being used as a public park, has attracted the interest of developers as a possible site for a building development.

A long-established neighbourhood is thus being threatened by changes that will destroy its character. A planning inquiry has been estab-lished to deal with the proposals suggested by the developers.

In any planning development, there are in-terest groups, who for various reasons, have a stake in the outcome of the project. Some of these groups are watching out for the interests of the general public; some are anxious to preserve a way of life; and others are motivated by the opportu-nity to make a profit. In this activity, you are given a role to play in a planning inquiry. You must present an argument supporting your position to the inquiry. The planning inquiry will make the final decision as to which of three proposals will be approved.

**Figure 23.1
A historically important home threatened by development.**

# What Should Be Done with the Cannon Estate?

A house of some historical importance has been purchased by a developer. The house is situated on a large sloping property in an attractive residential area of a large city. The property borders on a major arterial road, which is heavily used, particularly during the morning and evening rush hours. The developer has come up with three proposals:

**Proposal A**: This plan calls for the construction of eight single-family residences. These prestige homes would be carefully designed by architects to enhance rather than overwhelm the existing neighbourhood of modest detached houses. The historic building, described by the developer as being of minor historical significance, is to be torn down.

**Proposal B**: The emphasis in this proposal is on a mixed land use for this valuable piece of real estate. This plan suggests that the historical home be renovated as a commercial building for professional and medical offices. Surrounding the home and spilling down the slope, there would be an 18-unit luxury townhouse development.

**Proposal C**: This proposal calls for the restoration of the historical home on the property. The size of the building has made it difficult for the family to maintain it adequately. The building, once restored to its mid-1800s condition, will be used as a much-needed cultural centre for the community.

 Groups of students are to make presentations for the interest groups who have decided to appear before the planning inquiry. These concerns are outlined below:

| Group | Concerns |
|---|---|
| **Social Services Department** (local municipality) | ◆ preservation of family nature of the neighbourhood<br><br>◆ provision of much-needed additional housing |
| **Developer** | ◆ to develop new projects<br>◆ to maximize profits<br>◆ to maintain good standing in the community |
| **Traffic Commissioner** | ◆ minimization of traffic on the already overloaded arterial road<br>◆ efficient and safe ingress/egress for property |

| **Planner** (municipality) | ◆ can play a "kingmaker" role<br>◆ to be flexible in approach; not to show a preference<br>◆ to defend good planning; to see the benefits of all three proposals and to criticize poor or incomplete planning |
|---|---|
| **Neighbourhood Group # 1** | ◆ to increase the real estate values of their property<br>◆ to help the neighbourhood acquire an upscale status |
| **Neighbourhood Group # 2** | ◆ to retain the character of the neighbourhood<br>◆ to enjoy the quiet prestige of a historical estate in their midst |
| **Politicians** | ◆ to be sensitive to the wishes of voters<br>◆ to increase the tax base of the neighbourhood, best achieved through increased density or a mix of land uses<br>◆ to "roll with the punches," that is, to be swayed by good arguments |
| **Historical Society** | ◆ preservation of historical buildings<br>◆ limited tolerance for renovation as opposed to restoration |

The planning inquiry board, in whose hands the fate of the site rests, is composed of your teacher and two or four students. The teacher serves as the chairperson. While the various groups are working on their presentations, the members of the planning inquiry board circulate freely among the groups, sitting in on discussions, and probing for information that will help them arrive at a final decision. Here is the planning inquiry process:

## 1. *Preparation of Arguments*

After the class is divided into the various interest groups, a period of fifty to seventy-five minutes is to be spent preparing arguments to be presented to the planning inquiry members.

## 2. *Presentations*

Each group is allowed a maximum of five minutes to make their presentation.

## 3. *Rebuttals*

Once all the presentations have been heard, there will be an opportunity for rebuttals, to be moderated by the chairperson.

## 4. *Recess*

Once all the rebuttals have been heard, a recess will be held, during which regrouping and lobbying can take place. Groups may wish to ally themselves with other groups to present a stronger position as they try to influence the planning inquiry. Joint statements may be made by these new alliances during the next stage.

## 5. *Final Statements*

At this stage, final appeals can be made by individual groups or from alliances formed during the recess. These final statements should be limited to a maximum of one minute.

## 6. *The Decision*

In presenting their final decision that will settle the fate of the property in question, the planning inquiry members must address the reasons for their choice as well as their reasons for rejecting the other two proposals. Attempts must be made to appease all of the parties represented at the hearing.

# Developing a Plan for the Cannon Estate

## Materials

Site map of the Cannon Estate *(Blackline Master 23.1)*

1. Once a decision has been reached in favour of one of the three proposals, you are asked to put all the arguments behind you and assume the role of planner/designer. In this part of the assignment you prepare a plan or design for the use of the property based on the decision reached by the planning inquiry.
2. Use the site map provided (BLM 23.1) to prepare your work. Be sure to take into account the concerns of the surrounding neighbourhood, the orientation of the site, and the location of the main arterial road serving the site.

## Further Study

1. Identify and then prepare a study of a historical home in your community. Gather as much information as you can about the home from archival materials and interviews. Include as the main focus a photographic history of the home taken at different stages in the growth of the community up to the present day. Comment on the growth of urban development around the home at each stage.
2. Identify a historic home in your community or neighbourhood that may be in jeopardy by the end of this century because of urban development. Create an illustrated map of urban development projections to prove your point. Explain your position to others in a small group setting.
3. What advice would you offer to owners of historic homes in your community? Would you follow that advice if you unexpectedly inherited one of these homes? Why or why not?

BLM
23.1

# Integrative Studies

# Conformity and Individuality in the City

## 24

Because of their size, large urban centres at times can make people feel insignificant and anonymous. Sometimes it is easier for urban dwellers to conform to what the city considers normal and acceptable patterns of behaviour in order to feel they belong to the urban scene. In the residential areas, for example, homeowners follow acceptable property standards, maintaining the appearance of their home on a par with the homes of their neighbours.

As much as we conform, however, we still like to express our individuality, even if it is only in small ways. In residential areas of similar architectural styles, for instance, there will be differences in the colour of brick or paint. There may be a difference in the types of shrubbery and other plants surrounding the houses. Though the landscape pattern of each house may look similar, there are always individual differences if you examine the houses closely.

In some municipalities in parts of the world there are laws that require a rigid pattern of conformity. For example, in some Swiss cities the rooftops of buildings must be of a uniform style and colour to preserve the historic appearance of the city.

In this activity, you will have an opportunity to research examples of conformity and individuality in your community.

**Figure 24.1 Design of a suburban residential area. What factors contribute to the design of this urban community?**

Figure 24.2 *The Rebel*, Mordillo cartoon. Comment on the point being made in this cartoon.

# Analysing Conformity and Individuality in Your Community

1. With a partner, select any two of the following categories:
   (a) landscape architecture
   (b) transportation
   (c) commercial architecture
   (d) residential architecture
   (e) green space architecture
   (f) human interaction in an urban area

2. Chart five examples in your community of how people conform in each of your two categories. Compare your results.

3. Chart five examples in your community of how people demonstrate individuality in each of your two categories. How do these compare?

4. Discuss and develop a class list that everyone can agree to for each of the six categories under the headings "Ways in Which We Conform" and "Ways in Which We Express Our Individuality."

## Conclusion

1. Divide the class into six groups—an expert group for each category. In either a written or a visual form, display the information developed by the class in the class lists. You might consider using a poster collage format or making a photo or slide presentation to the class.

## Further Study

1. Construct a survey to assess the lifestyle of the inhabitants of an area in your neighbourhood. Include such lifestyle features as family size and composition, career focus concerns, leisure time activities, and so forth. Display your findings in the form of a graph.

2. How would our cities look if everyone was a conformist? an individualist?

# The Architects' Show
# –Renovation on a Grand Scale

## 25

Perhaps at some time you have considered how you would like to redecorate or renovate your room or your home. Think what it would be like if you had a chance to renovate or completely redesign a whole area of the town or city where you live. What would you eliminate and what would you add? You might like to draw from city plans and distinctive architecture of great world cities or you might develop your own look—ancient, modern, or fantasy. In this activity you have the chance to exercise your imagination.

## Redesigning a Community

## Materials

Bristol board
Tracing paper or sheets of Mylar
Templates for building sketches (*Blackline Master 25.1*)
Templates for building three-dimensional models of buildings (*Blackline Master 25.2*)
Property maps of your area (These can often be purchased at minimal cost from the city planning or central mapping departments of a municipality. They can be useful for planning, as they indicate the outlines of existing buildings.)

You have been asked to join with a partner to redesign 16 square blocks of your community. Your completed design can be entered in a class Architects' Show competition.

1. With your partner, choose an area of approximately 16 blocks. Depending on the size of your community and the size of your class, there may be some overlap of the areas being studied.
2. If possible, take a field trip to the area you have chosen. Determine:
   (a) the uses of the buildings in your sector;
   (b) the land uses needed in this area.
   Record this information in a journal or notebook.
3. Discuss with your partner how you might redesign the area.
4. Make two drawings on separate sheets of paper: one drawing to be an overhead view of the area based on a property map overview, the other to be a side view (profile) of a street scene in the area. Try to create a three-dimensional effect in your drawings. You can use the sheet of city building shapes (BLM 25.1) for inspiration.
5. Include a sketch map of the layout of the area's streets, with their names.
6. Name your redesigned area, adding a subtitle that will indicate its main intersection.
7. On a single sheet of paper, write an explanation to support your design plan.
8. Prepare a legend with a colour code to indicate building and open space details in your drawings.
9. Mount the drawings and the write-up on a sheet of Bristol board.

## Conclusion

1. If your class has decided on a competition, the Architects' Show can be graded by all those involved, as well as by teachers and students from other classes over a three- to five-day period. The designs are graded out of a possible 30 marks. Create a scorecard from the listing of criteria to consider. Note that each item has a maximum value of 5 points for a possible total of 30 points. The average score of all the ballots tabulated for your design will produce your score for the activity.

> **Criteria to Consider for Evaluating Displays**
>
> ♦ Visual impact *(5 points)*
> ♦ Written explanation *(5 points)*
> ♦ Neatness *(4 points)*
> ♦ Use of space *(5 points)*
> ♦ Originality of design *(6 points)*
> ♦ Compatibility *(5 points)*

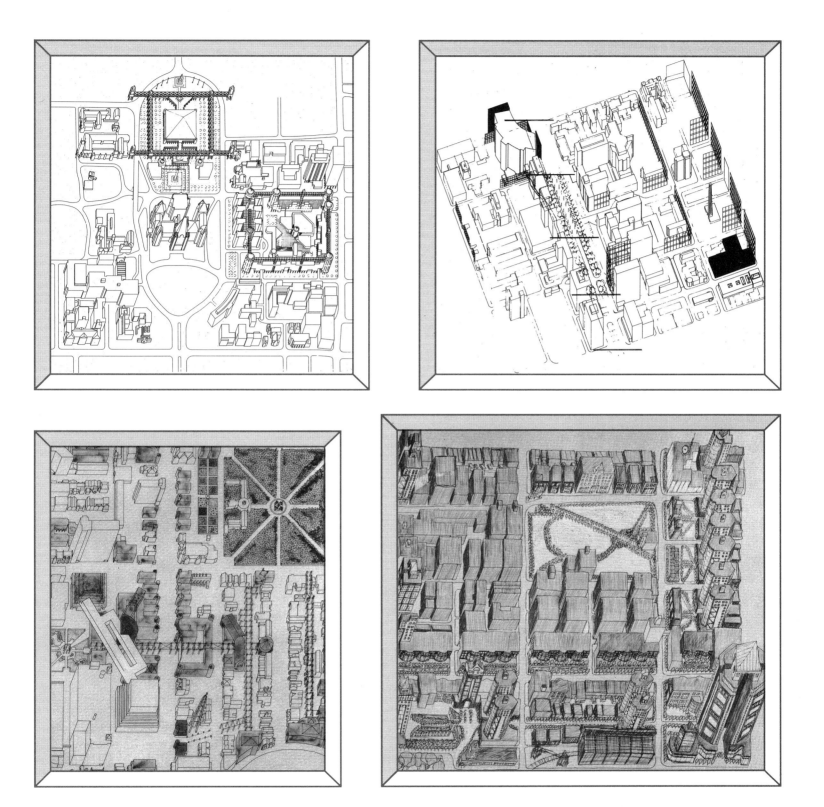

Figure 25.1 Sections of a city redesigned. Here and on page 82 is part of an exhibition in which various architects/planners redesigned sections of a city.

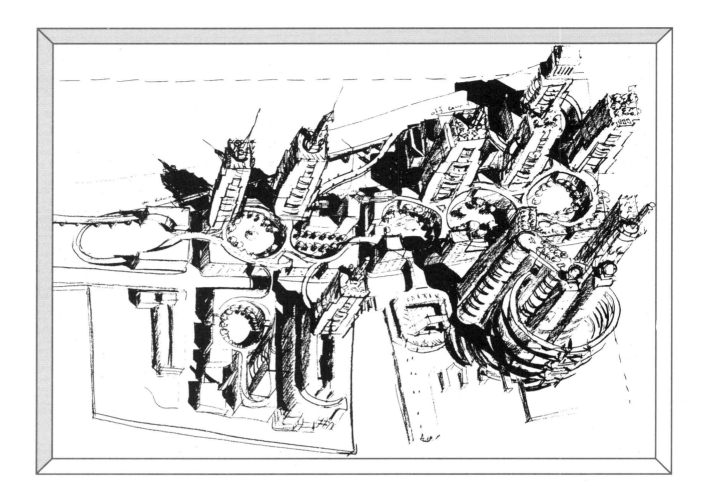

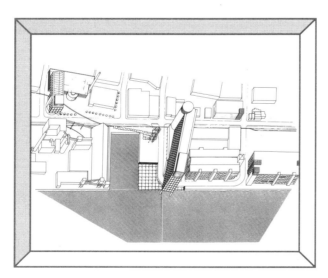

## Further Study

1. Create a three-dimensional construction model of your community using the set of eight templates provided (BLM 25.2).
2. What function do these architectural reconstructions serve in urban communities?
3. Collate, over a period of a month, articles about similar redesign in your local area. Present your findings to a small group with a view to actively encouraging a familiarity with the growth of your community.
4. What sort of career opportunities do such urban endeavours support in your urban centre? Brainstorm in a small group. Then, invite a representative sampling of individuals from selected careers into your class to find out more about their professions and to share your Architect Show redesigns.

# The Shape of Cities

H igh up in an airplane we can easily recognize the cluster patterns of our cities, their grey-coloured buildings, and often the polluted haze that covers most large urban centres like a dome. The distinctive shapes of cities are also clearly seen from this bird's eye perspective, as are urban growth patterns and constraints. If we were able to trace the outlines of these images, they could be useful in helping us understand the factors that determine the shapes our cities assume.

Cities grow as more and more people come to live there, drawn by the amenities the city has to offer. Within the city, these amenities tend to be concentrated around a central focal point–the "heart of the city" or the central business district (CBD). It is from the CBD that the city radiates outward as it grows and changes its shape.

What is it that determines the direction this growth will take as the city develops? This activity focusses on those factors that shape our cities. In the assignment you examine the outline shapes of three urban centres, which provide clues to the physical landscape that surrounds each city site. The outlines should also provide visual clues as to the directions of future growth of these cities, which can be useful in predicting land use and investment possibilities.

# What Shapes Our Cities?

## Materials

Coloured pens or pencils
Atlas

1. Sketch two copies of the outlines you can perceive of each urban centre from the aerial views (Figures 26.1–26.3).
2. At the top of each page, write the name of the city.
3. On the top outline of each city, locate the CBD and mark the growth directions outward from the CBD, using arrows. Number each arrow.
4. Account for each arrow (growth direction), listing the determining factors. Consult an atlas to assist you in this process.
5. On the second outline of each city, draw in the factors that caused the city to grow in those directions.

6. Indicate in green on the overlay what you think will most likely be the next growth direction. Write reasons for your choice.
7. Indicate in red on the overlay where you think growth is least likely to occur. Write reasons for these constraints to future growth. In some cases it is very obvious what has controlled the growth pattern. It may be a natural constraint, for example, the sea or a mountain range. It may also be one created by society, for example, a green belt that restricts development or a political boundary.

*Top of the page is North.*

**Figure 26.1 An aerial view of Regina, Saskatchewan.**

**Figure 26.2 An aerial view of Moncton, New Brunswick.**

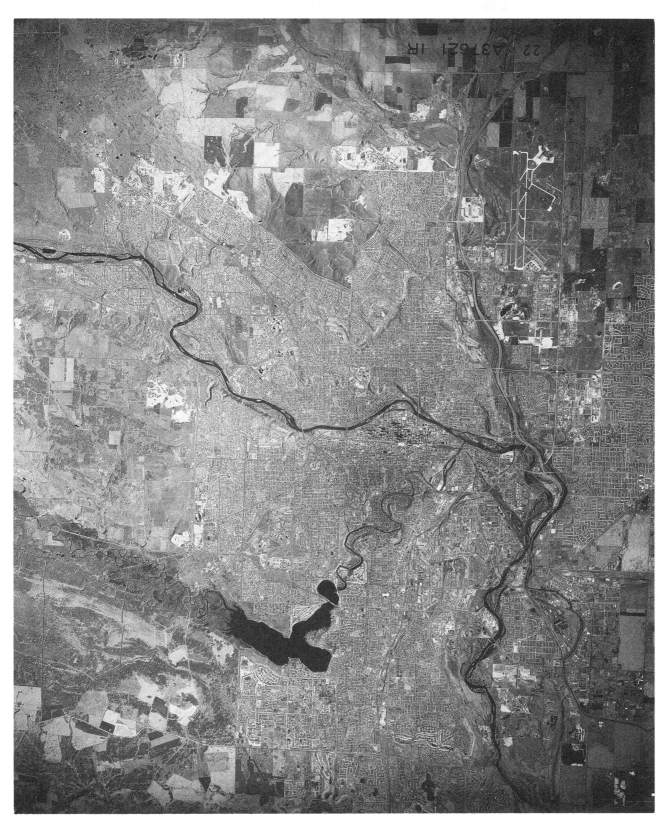

*Top of the page is North.*

Figure 26.3 An aerial view of Calgary, Alberta.

## Further Study

1. Research other aerial views and draw the outline shapes of some other of the world's famous cities.
2. Are certain cities easily recognizable by their shapes? Discuss.

# On the Grow —Small-Town Planning

# 27

The Planning Council has just received some great news: Minortown has been chosen from the five towns under consideration to be the site of a large new foreign automobile assembly plant.

The present 15 000 population of Minortown is comfortably settled between the old mill river and the crossroads. Conservative estimates indicate that the town will quadruple in size in the next ten years. The good news about the new industrial plan is therefore tempered by the reali-

zation that planning for the needs of the newcomers can impose a tremendous burden on the town. The town council has already been approached by many other interested parties wanting to purchase land in and around Minortown. This has prompted concerned residents and the town planners to develop a blueprint for the town's development. In this activity you can play a part in deciding how Minortown's development should proceed.

Figure 27.1 Richmond Hill, Ontario, 1900. A small town on the grow.

# Development in Minortown

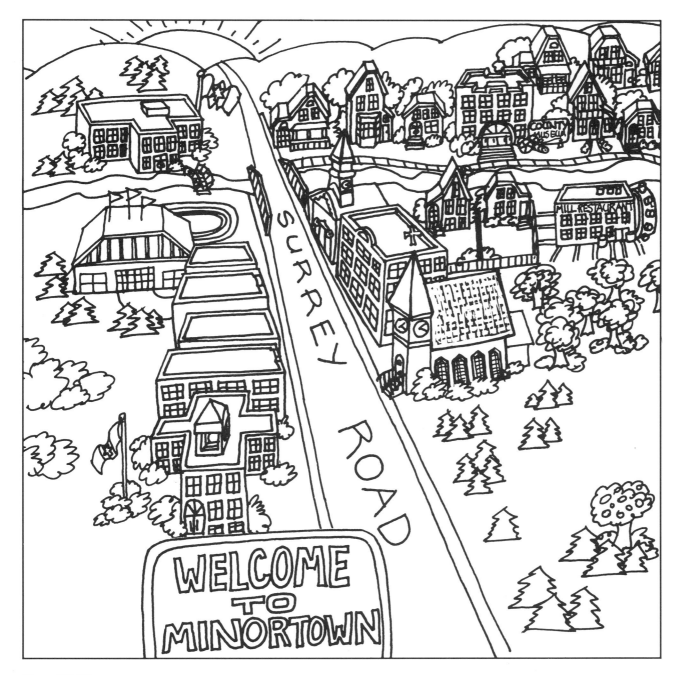

**Figure 27.2 Minortown.**

## Description of Minortown

Minortown is located on Surrey Road, approximately 0.5 km northwest of the crossroads of Surrey Road and Major Harris Road. The focal point, the peak market area of the town, is the town hall, situated between St. Paul's Church and St. Michael's Church. The town supports a community centre, two elementary schools, and a commercial strip area along Surrey Road. An old residential area has been well maintained along the river bank in the vicinity of the Mill Restaurant and Museum. The railway line has formed a link between the market to the west and the industrial sector of Minortown. Farm produce has been sold at the Crossroads Market for over one hundred years.

### Materials

Base map of Minortown (*Blackline Master 27.1*)
Peak market land value chart (*Blackline Master 27.2*)
Description of Minortown

### Preparation

Before any decision can be made:

1. Indicate the following developments on the base map of the town (BLM 27.1).
   (a) The Crown Land area to the southwest has recently been declared a National Park. These six squares are numbered A0, A1, B0, B1, C0 and C1.
   (b) The Province owns land in the northeast corner. This stand of forest will remain untouched and undeveloped. These four squares are numbered H6, H7, G6, and G7.
   (c) The old industrial sector from the late 1800s located along the river is also connected to the railway line (BLM 27.1).
   (d) Located on either side of the old industrial sector are two old residential areas. One boasts very expensive housing and a pleasant view, while the other provides simple accommodation for workers in the industries (BLM 27.1).
   (e) The non-resident automobile assembly plant has already purchased the land (D1, E1) south of Minortown at a total cost of $8.25 million. It has direct rail access and access to Major Harris Road.
2. Develop a legend as you proceed to identify the land uses on the map.

# Laying Out the Blueprint Plan

Minortown wishes to control the future growth that will take place in the area. The planning council has organized the submissions made by prospective developers in order of priority. As each submission is considered, in sequence, by the planning council members, determine how you would allocate the land on your base map of Minortown (BLM 27.1).

### Submission 1
Competition for the most accessible square is fierce. Every land developer has expressed an interest, and this interest has sparked a bidding war. Three major department stores have pooled their money to purchase this square at a total cost of $9 million.

### Submission 2
Several financial institutions have expressed interest in this same square, but are willing to settle for one other square which will allow access to both major roads and the nearby train station. Office towers will be constructed on this square. The cost of the development will be $6.75 million per square.

### Submission 3
The Province recognizes the need for a regional university and offers $4.25 million for a square. It must have access to a main road. A picturesque setting along the river has been suggested.

### Submission 4
A developer is willing to spend $4 million for each square of land available to build superior-quality, single-family homes. The developer has asked to purchase the best six squares of available land.

### Submission 5
A developer representing a commercial group wishes to purchase land to build a 125-store commercial shopping plaza for suburban residents. This group is willing to pay a total of $4.45 million for the best available square. This land must be located on either Major Harris Road or Surrey Road fairly close to the crossroads.

### Submission 6
A high tech manufacturing company is willing to pay $2.5 million for a square of land on either major road.

**Submission 7**

Another developer wishes to purchase eight squares for the purpose of building moderately priced single-family homes. This developer is willing to spend $2 million for each square of land.

**Submission 8**

Some other developers are willing to spend $7 million for two squares of land that have direct access to either main road. As the land is to be developed for an industrial park, these two squares must abut each other.

**Submission 9**

The city council has decided to donate a square of land for a city park near the city centre.

**Submission 10**

New industrial development and expansion on the existing industrial square is warranted. The developers are willing to expand onto a square that has direct rail access alongside the original industrial zone at a cost of $4.25 million.

**Submission 11**

Other developers are willing to spend $6 million for the best available land closest to the crossroads and the established town for the purpose of building high-rise condominiums and rental apartments.

**Submission 12**

The town will provide, at 50% of the land value, a square of land with access to both main roads to be developed as a downtown hospital and medical centre. The cost will be $3.35 million. The need for these services warrants the reduction in the land price.

**Submission 13**

Two squares of land will be donated for the development of a zoo. These squares will provide a quiet, tranquil location for the display and preservation of various species of the animal kingdom.

**Submission 14**

Special approval from the Planning Council has allowed the provision of two central squares to be developed as a secondary school site and a community centre. Direct access to either Major Harris Road or Surrey Road is necessary for at least one square. The community centre will house an indoor ice rink, a pool, and squash, racquetball, and basketball courts. The cost of the two squares of land has been set at $12 million.

**Submission 15**

A total of twelve squares of moderately-priced suburban housing have been set aside for developers at a cost of $1.5 million per square.

**Submission 16**

Two community parks with sports facilities should receive approval for the suburban areas at a cost of $2 million each.

**Submission 17**

The Planning Council has been asked to approve the sale of land at $2.5 million each per square for the following: three elementary schools, two police stations, two fire halls, four religious institutions, and two cemeteries.

**Submission 18**

The town council approved the sale of land at a total cost of $6.25 million for one water treatment plant on the river and four separate dump sites (five squares in all).

Any remaining squares are to be marked as future development to be developed at the Planning Council's discretion. This will complete your master blueprint for the new larger city of Majortown.

## Conclusion

1. Compare the symbols you used on your map with those used by other Planning Council members in your class. Is it more difficult or easier to read the other planners' maps? Agree on appropriate symbols for the class to use in common for each different land use.

2. In order to calculate the peak market land value area, complete a copy of the Peak Market Land Value Cost Sheet. Fill in the squares of the matrix according to the land values at the time of the sale, using your corresponding map. Be sure to leave blank any squares of unknown value.
   (a) Does any pattern of land values emerge on your blueprint plan?
   (b) Where was the original peak land value area in Minortown?
   (c) Where is the peak market land value location now in the new city of Majortown?
   (d) In what direction has the location of the peak market land value moved?
   (e) Where is the peak market land value location in your community? Name the crossroads or intersection.
   (f) Predict the location of the next peak market land value location in your community.

## Further Study

1. (a) Choose one land use type that may not benefit from the Planning Council decisions you have made because of the way the land value will be affected by the decision. Write a letter to negotiate the reversal of the planning decision from one of the groups affected. Include your reasons, explaining the benefits and disadvantages as you see them.

   (b) Draft a petition aimed at halting this development.

   (c) Establish a panel to debate the pros and cons of this controversial planning decision, for example, the proposal to establish a downtown park. Have the class choose one blueprint plan. Form groups to represent one of the land use types from this plan. Discuss and debate the issue. Groups can ally themselves with other land use groups in favour of or against the plan. Hold a class vote to decide the outcome.

2. (a) Using the theoretical model of land values in Figure 27.3, what accounts for the discrepancies in the pattern of land values as you move away from the centre of peak market value?

   (b) Using the real world model in Figure 27.3, account for the troughs and peaks away from the normal curve of land values.

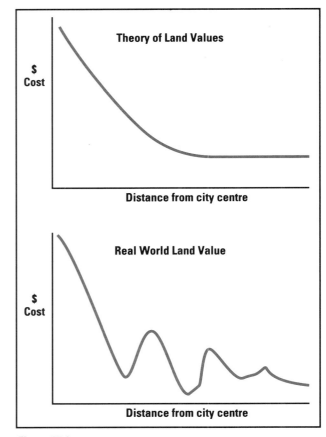

Figure 27.3

# Urban Park Design

Most urban centres provide a certain amount of parkland for their citizens. In this unit we consider the factors that affect the layout and design of urban parks, the many functions that parks provide, and the origins of parks in urban settings.

In ancient cities there was no reason to develop urban parklands, as open green space was no farther away than the city limits. However, as cities grew and the cities' boundaries moved farther outward, the need for park space closer to the heart of the city soon became evident. The rich were able and willing to create country-like

**Figure 28.1 Central Park, New York City.** Compare and contrast the use of park space with that of the surrounding city.

settings within their large estates, and would often allow the use of this land as park space. Parks offered a respite from the built-up urban environment. A simple walk in a park can provide the urban dweller with a much-needed change of pace from the stress of urban living.

The formal design of the fashionable parks found in Paris came about as a result of the demand for an escape from the city. It is said that prior to the creation of these public parks, Parisians would stroll, rest, and picnic in the cemeteries of the city. In fact, park design owes a great deal to the design of these early cemeteries.

Unfortunately, in spite of the obvious pleasures that parks afford their citizens, urban park space has not as a rule been a planning priority with city councils in the past. Many of today's parks, for example, exist only by chance.

The local park in your neighbourhood may exist because the land was donated to the city. Other parks exist because the land has been deemed unsuitable for building or prone to flooding and therefore has been designated as park space. More recently, parks have been planned to suit planning code requirements, which stipulate that a certain percentage of developed land must be green space.

Some green belt areas used to control urban sprawl provide examples of park space that have come about as a result of urban growth, not necessarily because of a concern about green space.

Active citizen groups have frequently protected green space from developers and maintained or created new urban parks.

# Creating Park Space in the City

Figure 28.2

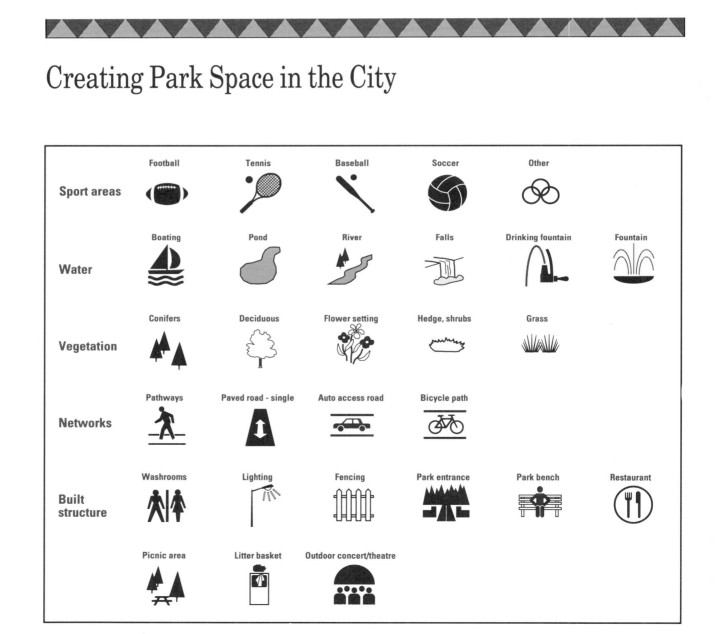

## Materials

Base map of park site (*Blackline Master 28.1*)

1. Using the symbols represented in Figure 28.2, on page 92, create a drawing on the base map (BLM 28.1) of a new park for the downtown core of an urban centre.
2. Prepare a one-page description of your park design.

## Conclusion

1. Your design will be evaluated by your peers or your teacher on the basis of the following criteria (2-5 marks each):
   ♦ access to the park
   ♦ compatibility with other factors
   ♦ aesthetics of your design
   ♦ degree of completeness
   ♦ neatness of presentation

### Factors to Consider for Your Park Design

1. How will you separate the urban environment from the park environment?
2. Remember to use the symbols according to the proper scale.
3. How efficient is your network of paths and roadways through the park?
4. How many park entrances will you include and how efficient are their locations?
5. Have you considered safety factors for children and adequate lighting?
6. Will there be any natural or constructed contours in your park?
7. Have you included formal or informal gardens in your design?
8. Have you considered the effects of traffic and the use of the park's sports facilities in planning quiet areas in the park?
9. Have you made use of water and water areas in your park design?

BLM 28.1

# Assessing the Value of Park Space

How can one place a value on Urban Park Space? Now that you have completed your designs you may wish to assess the parks in your local area. Here are some suggestions:

1. Ask representatives from your local parks department to visit your school and assess your urban park designs. Perhaps they could present their view of the value or need for urban park space.
2. Submit some of your park designs to the local planning department. Perhaps your designs could be converted to fit into a redesign project for a local park.
3. Interview local park visitors to gain further insight into the value of park space. Perhaps you could ask their reasons for visiting the park, the distance they have travelled, how often they visit the park and what they think would improve their park.

4. Park value can be assessed by measuring park use. You may wish to map the location of park visitors within the local park and note by what entrance or from what direction they enter and exit the park. A spatial mapping project of this sort can lead to some useful discussions on park use and park traffic.
5. Investigate the reasons behind your city planner's decision to assign park status to certain areas in your community. How do the parks in your urban centre become established?

## Further Study

1. Are there individuals in your community whose persistent political protests helped to protect and encourage the addition of more green space? What were their goals? What did they accomplish?

# Rooftop Design

n urban areas, space is usually very limited and urban space is relatively costly. At the same time there is a great amount of space in our urban areas that could be considered wasted space. To many, the space that we use for transportation is a collective waste, as are parking areas. Others think that open areas and parkland constitute wasted space. As you can see, the camps are firmly divided: people space versus industrial/mechanical space.

In urban centres we try to make the most of what we have, with areas going through periods of rejuvenation and renewal. There is, however,

one type of space that until recently has been overlooked. These are the rooftop areas of our buildings, which can provide useful and pleasant places in our cities. In this activity you have the opportunity to create a usable space from two different unused rooftop areas. One is the roof of a garage attached to a house. The other is the roof of a ten-storey apartment building surrounded by other tall buildings in the downtown core. You have been given approval by the city building inspectors to use this space as you see fit, as long as the structure is sound and drainage is not affected.

**Figure 29.1 Rooftop *Tennis* by Mordillo.**

# Living at the Top

## Materials

Scale drawing of house rooftop area (*Blackline Master 29.1*)

Scale drawing of apartment building rooftop area (*Blackline Master 29.2*)

1. Brainstorm with a small group to compile a variety of diverse uses/functions for a rooftop. Time limit: three to five minutes.
2. Choose only one of the two rooftops to design.
3. Complete the design, using the scale drawing of the rooftop you have chosen (BLM 29.1 or BLM 29.2). Use the symbol chart provided (Figure 29.2). You may include other uses for the roof as long as the scale of the material is appropriate.
4. Give your design a title.
5. Your submission should be accompanied by a written description, listing five benefits that this design provides to the owner of the property.

### Factors to Consider for Rooftop Design

♦ Consider the design items shown in Figure 29.2 as possible features you might incorporate in your rooftop design.

♦ For the space to be useful, consider privacy, noise reduction, circulation (movement) patterns, and natural weather phenomena.

♦ Consider how many ways the rooftop area can be used.

♦ Safety is an important consideration in any rooftop design.

## Conclusion

1. After the designs have been completed, vote on the top five designs in each of the two categories in your class. Before you cast your vote, consider as an example the criteria shown below. To facilitate scoring, ensure that everyone uses the same criteria. Assign a maximum of 5 points in each category with a maximum allowable total of 20 points.

### Sample Criteria for Judging Rooftop Designs

♦ Originality of design

♦ Attractiveness of the presentation

♦ Flexible and creative use of space

♦ Cost effectiveness of design

## Further Study

1. Redesign the rooftop, an atrium, or the grassed area in and around your school as a class project. Submit the proposal to your principal and arrange to have the plan displayed in the main hallway or the office.
2. Consider other urban areas that could be redesigned to make them more useful. Compile a list.
3. How can rooftop redesign enhance urban living?

Figure 29.2

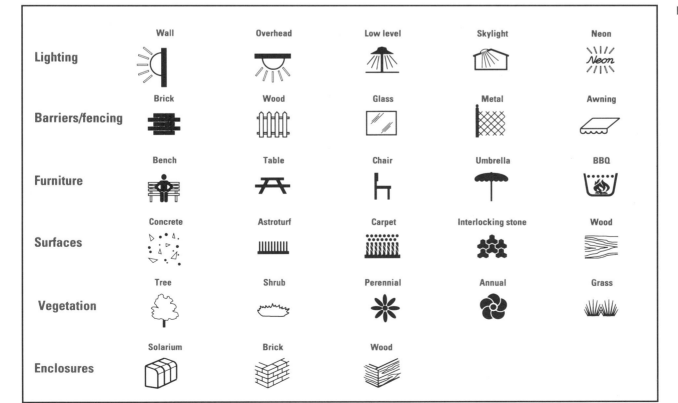

# Landscape Design

The appearance of most buildings can be enhanced by attractive settings. A finished house benefits from the framing of well-designed property around it. This can be accomplished by landscape design. Landscape architects are the professionals who lay out patterns of natural vegetation to improve the appearance of buildings. In centuries past, landscape architects often designed property for wealthy clients on a very grand scale to create a vista, a long view, something that was visually pleasing. The gardens of the palace at Versailles outside Paris in France are one famous example of a seventeenth- and-eighteenth-century use of landscape design to enhance the property of kings. Natural groundcovers, flowers, trees and shrubs, as well as fountains, statues, and even other buildings, can be used to give a property a visual framework.

**Figure 30.1 Versailles Gardens near Paris, France. Why would this design be classified as formal?**

On a smaller scale, residential buildings with limited grounds can also make use of the landscape architect's skills. This was not always the case in urban centres. Traditionally only the very wealthy could ever afford to use urban property to create a natural setting. This accounts for the lack of green space within older European cities, where buildings were designed to abut against one another. Any undeveloped city property or natural open space in the city was considered wasted space. After all, one had only to walk a short distance to the nearby outskirts of the city to enjoy a natural setting. Today, especially in the younger cities of North America, people can enjoy the luxury of more open space surrounding their homes. However, as land values in cities rise steeply, large house lots may again become a luxury and people may have to reconsider the relative importance of having natural areas around their homes.

In this activity you have the opportunity to play the role of the landscape architect in one of the following three projects.

Figure 30.2 Street scene, Rye, East Sussex, England. What opportunities exist to enhance this scene with landscaping?

Figure 30.3 Japanese garden. What features are characteristic of this landscape style?

# How Does Your Garden Grow?

## Materials

Base maps of three lot plans (*Blackline Masters 30.1 and 30.2*)

1. Choose one property from the following three areas to be designed:
   (a) The front and back of a suburban house built in the 1950s on a 15 m wide lot (BLM 30.2).
   (b) The front and back of a 70-year-old house on a typical downtown lot with an 8 m frontage (BLM 30.1).
   (c) The front and back of a recently built town-house with a 6 m width (BLM 30.1).
2. Plot your landscape design on the base map grid. Consult the illustrations of plants and landscaping materials and furniture in Figure 29.2 for ideas and symbols to use.

---

**Factors to Consider in Landscape Design**

◆ Consider the rules of balance and composition. (Consult your school's art department for help.)

◆ Decide on a plan that harmonizes with the building's architectural style.

◆ Consider how to ensure that the landscape features take priority.

◆ Familiarize yourself with local climatic conditions. The climate in your area may eliminate certain landscape choices.

---

## Conclusion

1. (a) Which of the three projects proved the most difficult? the most rewarding?
   (b) What restrictions did you encounter with your project?
   (c) Guesstimate the amount of time that would be necessary to complete each of these landscaping projects if the designs were acceptable to the property owners. Check the accuracy of your guess by consulting about price with a local landscape expert.
2. Study all the plans to assess what the most popular ground covers, shrubs, trees, etc. were. Rank the popularity of each.

## Further Study

1. As a class or large group, draw a new design for the landscape surrounding your school.
2. Consider the place where you live and suggest improvements you could make to the landscape surrounding your residence, or a small garden for an apartment balcony or condominium complex.
3. Compile a slide presentation of interesting landscape designs in your community.
4. Invite a local landscaper into your class. Before the visit, form small groups and develop a list of questions based on landscape design topics. Consider a framework for your topic headings which address what a day in the life of a landscaper is all about.

# Planning a House on a Small Urban Lot

With the fast-rising land costs in most urban places, architects and planners are increasingly challenged to put more functional design in less space. In this activity you are asked to design an urban house on a small lot. The challenge is to provide a functional efficient home of architectural and aesthetic merit in a limited area.

Figure 31.1
Contemporary detached house on a narrow lot. Contrast this form of architecture to suburban bungalows where land is less expensive.

# Designing a Narrow House

## Materials

Site map of urban lot (*Blackline Master 31.1*)

1. Using the specifications given below and the site map, design a dwelling to be erected on the site. In addition to the site map, your design should include at least one elevation drawing and floor plans.

### Specifications for Residential Plan
**Area of lot:** 400 m²
**Width:** 10 m
**Depth:** 40 m
**Occupants:**
    Family of four: parents in mid-forties
                       boy, 14 years old
                       girl, 10 years old
**Open space:** 35%, as required by municipal bylaw
**Height:** 3 storeys maximum
**Parking:** one-car garage required

## Conclusion

1. What rooms become more compact and integrated as a result of limited space? Explain your rationale.
2. Study the new home design plans advertised in newspapers and featured in specialty home magazines. Over a period of a few weeks, collate a representational sampling of new home designs. What trends in housing does your sampling suggest for your urban community?

## Further Study

1. What do you predict will be the average model home design for the year 2010? Survey a few real estate agents to compare predictions.
2. Assess the viability of the *Grow House* described in the newspaper article.

BLM 31.1

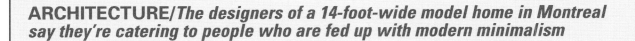

# ARCHITECTURE/*The designers of a 14-foot-wide model home in Montreal say they're catering to people who are fed up with modern minimalism*

(BY STEPHEN GODFREY
Quebec Bureau)

A model home on view at McGill University until June 30 has been hailed as a prototype for affordable housing of the future, but it's also a conscious attempt to return to architectural tradition.

Called the Grow Home, because it can be added to and subdivided according to the owner's needs, the 14-foot-wide, 1,000-square-foot house would cost only $65,000 to build in downtown Montreal, compared to the current average of $110,000 for a new home in the city. Witold Rybczynski and Avi Friedman, both professors at the McGill School of Architecture, say their design harks back to an era before restrictive zoning and building regulations prevented construction of such a narrow house. But, according to a newspaper report this week, city officials will meet with the two architects to consider changing the zoning bylaws that prohibit building houses under 18 feet in width. (Other Canadian cities, most notably Ottawa, already permit such narrow townhouses.)

A row house, of the type most common in older cities such as Boston, Philadelphia and Montreal, the Grow Home also attempts to be a generic classic dwelling. Such elements as the Georgian-style strip of molding over the front door, the mullioned windows, the dormer roof, the French doors leading out from the living room onto a small pergola suggest that modern architecture—or, in some cases, modern zoning—isn't what first-time homebuyers need now.

Rybczynski, the author of the architectural bestseller, Home, maintains that the average person's taste in housing is conservative, and the Grow Home follows this principle. "We couldn't afford to do an authentic style," he says, "but we didn't want to make it a piece of machinery. A lot of modern architects stripped everything away, and people have reacted against that minimalism." Rybczynski's most recent book, The Most Beautiful House in The World, traces the building of his own conservatively styled house outside Montreal.

A number of developers are among the 6,000 visitors to the display, and Friedman says he is confident that, in five years, "you will see projects that originated with the ideas in this house. I say this because some of these developers are bringing their draftsmen with them."

Because it uses existing materials and simple shapes, the Grow Home concept cannot be patented, but neither man expresses regret at not gaining financially if the project is imitated. Rybczynski points out that many of the restrictions that would make the Grow Home impossible to build were drafted in an era when suburban land was cheap, and legislators could demand minimum lot sizes to encourage large houses. Similarly, narrow lots were associated with inferior lighting and, in the days before artificial ventilation, poor air circulation.

Also, as Rybczynski pointed out in an article for Canadian Architect, 56 per cent of families in the late fifties had three or more children, whereas the figure has fallen to 20 per cent. Today, more than a third of all families only have one child. The need for large houses is not as great -- even if the taste for big rooms has not disappeared.

The two professors have learned of those tastes, and the potential market of the house, since the Grow Home opened on June 6. Isolated on a plot of grass in the heart of McGill's campus and surrounded by large stone and concrete buildings, the Grow Home (this version, called the Windsor, is one of five variations the pair designed) has the fragility of a cutout or a dollhouse to some onlookers.

"Some people are surprised how big it is on the inside, compared to the impression given by the exterior," says Rybczynski. "Yet other people who live in apartments have this idea that a house has to be much bigger. One couple commented that you couldn't go up the stairs side by side, even though our stairway is standard width."

"The two groups who seemed most interested to me were the younger people from, say, the Plateau Mont-Royal area, when you tell them they can have the house for the $500-700 they're already paying in rent," says Friedman. "And then there are the seniors, who live now in a large home and are thinking of something more compact."

At a time when many North American city cores, including Montreal, are losing population to the suburbs, the Grow Home tries to be a blend of both settings, says Rybczynski. "The line between urban and suburban is blurring. Land is more expensive in the suburbs, while cities have to be more suburban in their use of green space."

If consumers' tastes are conservative, and developers, according to a study by the American Department of Housing and Urban Development, take three to nine years to accept innovation, is it possible that the Grow Home is too ahead of its time to be accepted by buyers accustomed to bigger houses? "We may be too early for that change," says Rybczynski with a smile, "but we're certainly not too late."

# Designing a Solar Residence

*32*

Solar energy is free for the taking, inexhaustible and environmentally clean. Individuals often feel there is little they can do personally in terms of energy conservation and environmental clean-up. However, making use of the low-grade heat of the sun can decrease the cost of home heating and reduce the need to burn fossil fuels. This is an option developers are slowly beginning to incorporate into their housing designs.

In order to take full advantage of the sun as an energy source, a radical change must occur in the architecture of buildings. The inclusion of solar energy collecting devices in the design of the building need not detract from the attractiveness of the structure itself. In the hands of a sensitive architect/designer, a solar home can provide a bright, comfortable space in which to live.

In the first part of this activity, the concept of passive solar architecture is examined as it is used in an actual working solar residence. In the second part, you will be asked to design a solar dwelling of your own in an urban setting.

Solar energy can be captured by *active* and *passive* means. The two approaches are quite different and use opposing technological methods.

**Passive solar gain** occurs when the actual solar collection is integrated into the design of the building. Relying on natural convection currents to move the warmed air, there is usually little additional energy needed to heat the building. Passive solar gain systems are difficult to incorpo-

**Figure 32.1
Millard House,
Lake Simcoe,
Ontario.**

rate into existing buildings, although the addition of a sunroom in a home is often an attempt to take advantage of passive solar gain.

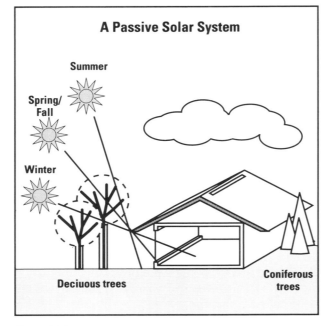

**A Passive Solar System**

Summer

Spring/Fall

Winter

Deciuous trees

Coniferous trees

Figure 32.2

**Active solar gain** is a system in which an antifreeze fluid is pumped (hence "active") from rooftop collectors to the interior of the building. This system, which involves an energy input, tends to be more complicated and is subject to breakdowns. However, this type of system can be retrofitted to an existing building.

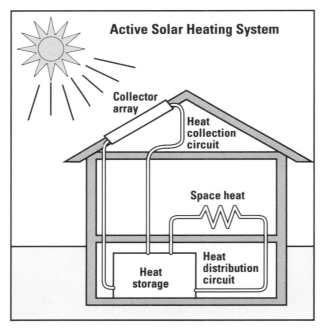

**Active Solar Heating System**

Collector array

Heat collection circuit

Space heat

Heat distribution circuit

Heat storage

Figure 32.3

The passive solar gain philosophy was used in the design and construction of the Millard solar residence on the shore of Lake Simcoe. Peter Millard, a technical consultant in the automotive industry, had been aware of the energy-saving potential in solar designs for some time. After five years of accumulated research, an existing, 70-year-old summer cottage on the site was demolished, and in the fall of 1980, construction began on what was soon to be affectionately called the Sunhouse.

The description of the construction process and the design features of the Millard solar home helps to illustrate six basic principles of passive solar design. (See Figure 32.2.)

**Heat Sink**: Because the active collection of solar energy occurs only during the daylight hours, provision must be made to store the collected heat during the night. Traditionally, the materials used to store heat energy are stone, masonry, water, and concrete.

In the Millard residence, the heat sink function is performed in a number of ways:

• The downstairs solarium floor consists of interlocking brick over 61 cm of compacted sand.

• The Trombe Wall, consisting of a two-storey concrete block wall filled with sand, acts both as a heat collector and a heat sink. (See below for a further explanation of the Trombe Wall.)

• A simple but ingenious basement heat sink is also installed in the Millard solar house. As shown in Figure 32.2, an area 9 m x 7.5 m in the basement has a 75 mm galvanized downspout pipe in a 300 mm centre pattern set in the 200 mm concrete floor. Hot air from the solarium collecting area is blown into the basement floor, where it is stored and slowly released at night as radiant heat.

**Insulation**: Even with an effective heat sink, the heat must be trapped in the building by insulating material in the outside walls and roof; otherwise the heat will escape. The Sunhouse is "super-insulated." This means that insulation has been installed well above minimum building code requirements.

**Trombe Wall**: The Trombe Wall refers to a solid masonry wall placed immediately behind the glazing (glass) in a passive design. Incoming solar radiation penetrates the glass and is absorbed by the dark surface of the wall, just as there is a tremendous heat buildup in a closed car in direct sunlight in the summer. Although, ideally, the Trombe Wall is placed close to the glass, this is not always possible and is certainly not aesthetically pleasing. (In the Sunhouse, the Trombe Wall is placed 3 m from the glass to provide a pleasant sunroom or solarium.)

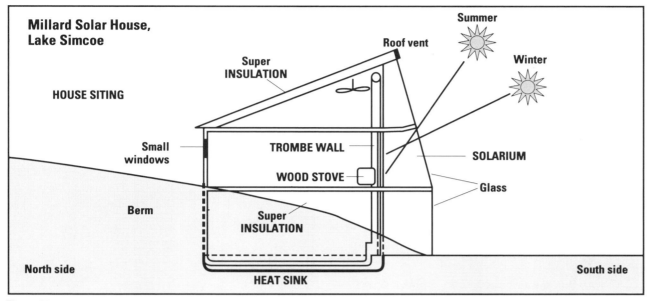

**Millard Solar House, Lake Simcoe**

HOUSE SITING

Super INSULATION

Small windows

TROMBE WALL

WOOD STOVE

Berm

Super INSULATION

North side

HEAT SINK

Roof vent

Summer

Winter

SOLARIUM

Glass

South side

Figure 32.4

The Trombe Wall aids in cooling the building in the summer as well as heating it in the winter months:

• In the winter season, the Trombe Wall provides direct solar gain through the solarium, and air circulates by convection with the assistance of a basement fan.

• In the summer season, the Trombe Wall acts as a "solar chimney." With the added heat buildup in the solarium in the summer months, the air rises and is released through roof vents. The Trombe Wall increases the upward flow of hot air and allows cool air from the shaded north side to enter the house, thus providing a natural air conditioner!

**Solarium**: This is the main collecting area of the solar house. The massive expanse of glass in the solarium gives passive solar houses their distinctive appearance.

The glass used in the Sunhouse is tempered Thermopane (air pocket insulation), and consists of seven 1 x 2 m panels on the main floor and ten 1 x 2 m panels on the lower level. The glass on the main level is set at a 78° angle for optimum winter heat gain.

The air heated in the solarium rises to the top of the solarium where it is drawn into a 450 mm plenum (air duct) to be delivered to the basement heat sink. The fan used to assist in this operation is controlled by an automatic thermostat.

Excess heat rises and is trapped in the peaked roof, where in summer it is released through roof vents. In the winter, another plenum draws the excess air into the basement heat sink.

**Supplementary Heat**: An airtight wood stove on the main floor with a fresh air intake helps heat the building during the winter months. The exposed chimney stack passes up through two storeys, helping to transfer heat to the surrounding air.

A small electric furnace in the basement is also connected to the air distribution system.

**House Siting**: Ideally, a building should face due south for maximum solar gain. (However, in the case of the Millard solar house, the building is 10° east of due south for site and lot size considerations.)

A berm on the north side of the building protects and insulates the rear of the structure and helps direct the cold northwesterly winds up over the building.

There are a minimum number of small windows on the north side of the structure to avoid undue heat loss.

The angle of the eaves prevents direct solar gain in the summer when the sun is high in the sky. In the winter months when the sun is low in the sky, solar gain is possible in spite of the overhanging eaves.

In terms of landscaping, it is preferable to have coniferous trees on the north side of the structure and deciduous trees on the south side.

# Assessing the Millard Sunhouse

1. The Millard solar residence is described as being superinsulated. How much insulation is normally used in the average house?
2. Why is the Trombe Wall described as acting as a "solar chimney"?
3. Is the Millard solar residence 100% passive? Explain.
4. Explain the choice of coniferous and deciduous trees, where specified.
5. The temperature data shown at the right was recorded on March 14, 1989. These temperatures were recorded inside the main living area of the Sunhouse, in the solarium, and outside.
   (a) Construct a multiline time graph to illustrate the change in temperature in the three locations.
   (b) At what time of day would it make sense to open the doors of the solarium to help warm up the inside of the house? Explain.
   (c) At what time of day should they be closed?
   (d) What happened to the outdoor temperature when the sun was blocked by cloud over?
   (e) What was the effect on the solarium temperature when the skies clouded over?
   (f) Why did the indoor temperatures remain so stable even though no supplementary heat was used during this time period?

| | INSIDE | SOLARIUM | OUTSIDE | Other |
|---|---|---|---|---|
| Time | Temp.°C | Temp.°C | Temp.°C | Factors |
| 7:00 a.m. | 21 | 10 | −4 | clear sunny skies |
| 8:00 a.m. | 21 | 13 | −4 | |
| 9:00 a.m. | 21 | 20.5 | −1 | |
| 10:00 a.m. | 22 | 27 | 2 | |
| 11:00 a.m. | 23 | 29 | 4 | |
| 12:00 noon | 25 | 33 | 7 | skies clouding over |
| 1:00 p.m. | 24 | 29 | 6 | |
| 2:00 p.m. | 24 | 31 | 6 | |
| 3:00 p.m. | 24 | 27 | 5 | |
| 4:00 p.m. | 23.5 | 24.5 | 4 | |
| 5:00 p.m. | 23 | 24 | 4 | |
| 6:00 p.m. | 21.5 | 22 | 4 | |
| 7:00 p.m. | 21 | 21 | 4 | |
| 8:00 p.m. | 20.5 | 18 | 4 | |
| 9:00 p.m. | 21 | 17 | 4 | |

# Designing a Solar Residence

## Materials

Copy of site map for solar design (*Blackline Master 32.1*)
Pencils and ruler
Although solar architecture can be pleasing and has undisputed environmental merits, incorporating this type of design into the existing urban fabric can be problematic. The aim tends to be to retain as many solar features as possible while not clashing visually with the other houses on the street. In this part of the assignment, you will be required to meet this challenge as you design a solar house of your own.

1. Examine the site map (BLM 32.1) carefully. The site is in a neighbourhood of turn-of-the-century two- and three-storey Victorian red and yellow brick dwellings. Many of these houses have bay windows.

2. Design the floor plan of your proposed solar dwelling. The design must:
   (a) incorporate the architectural character of the neighbourhood;
   (b) take into consideration the direction of maximum solar gain (south);
   (c) have a ground floor area of at least 200 m²;
   (d) include three or four bedrooms;
   (e) provide parking for at least one car.
3. Design, on graph paper or tracing paper, elevation sketches of your design.
4. Write a summary and defence of your design. Foamcore models and presentation boards can be used effectively to illustrate your ideas.

# Designing a
# Retirement Home

anada's population is growing older. In the early 1980s, approximately 10% of the country's population was over 65 years of age. This figure is expected to rise dramatically over the next few decades as the "baby boom" generation reaches retirement age. The social and economic implications of an aging population are enormous. In fact, *gerontology*, the study of aging, is one of the fastest-growing disciplines in colleges and universities worldwide.

One of the issues facing planners in the future will therefore be the provision of suitable housing for an older population. Although most older people prefer to stay in their own homes after retirement, this is not always possible. The need for support services, such as housekeeping, meal preparation, and personal health care services, means that alternative housing models must be found. Possible solutions include cooperatives, *granny flats*, home-sharing, and collective housing.

**gerontology**: Based on the Greek words *geron* (old man) and *logos* (reason), gerontology is the science of aging. It studies both the aging process of the individual as well as the social problems of the elderly.

**granny flats**: A granny flat consists of a portable modular cottage, which is placed on the property of the son or daughter of an older person. All services, such as telephone, water, electricity, and sewers, are connected to the main house. The concept, first attempted by the Australian Government in the mid-1970s, allows children to care for an older parent while, at the same time, providing the parent with a sense of privacy and independence.

Figure 33.1 True Davidson Retirement Home. Effective and creative use of a difficult landscape.

# Planning for the Future

## Materials

Site map for retirement home (*Blackline Master 33.1*)

This assignment involves the planning of an old-age retirement home on a given plot of land. In planning your building(s), many considerations specific to the needs of the elderly must be made. These are outlined in the Specifications for the Retirement Home.

In addition to the facilities mentioned in the specifications, the following factors should be considered in your design:

1. Create a modular construction design. This form of design is less expensive in that it can use prefabricated standard-sized units. Alternatively, modular construction can mean repeating the same basic design with minor variations over and over again. An excellent example of this is the honeycomb pattern of a beehive. The challenge in using this form of construction is to avoid monotony by arranging the units in an attractive fashion.
2. In designing your retirement home, keep in mind that the residents, although elderly, are independent and mobile. Provide opportunities for movement about the residence. Pedestrian traffic is a prime consideration in the design. The smooth and pleasant flow of pedestrian travel should be a main design factor.
3. Ready access should be available for service and delivery trucks. Provide a central service core that would help to amalgamate many of the common needs of the service functions of the residence, that is, water, sewers, ventilation, and waste disposal.
4. Provide a central area where residents could meet and gather. This area would be open, inviting and easily accessible. Its function would be similar to the "downtown" or village common in urban places. The lobby or main entrance area of the retirement home would be a suitable location for such a "main street."

## Conclusion

1. Discuss the social implications of long-range planning for an aging population. How does your design address this shift in demographics to an older population?
2. Make a class display of retirement designs. Evaluate the effectiveness of the retirement homes created.

## Further Study

1. What architectural layout features would you incorporate into a residence that served as a halfway house for young teenagers in need of home support? What aspects about this kind of residence are similar to those required by a retirement home? Explain why there are similarities.

### Specifications for the Retirement Home Design

| | |
|---|---|
| **Area of Lot**: | 1 ha |
| **Occupants**: | 250 residents: 150 female<br>100 male<br>Occupancy based on two persons per room |
| **Open Space**: | 30% is desired. This space is to consist of gardens, parkland, lawns, and wooded areas to form a "soft" landscape around or through the site. |
| **Height**: | A building(s) with a low elevation is desired, as a minimal number of stairs is preferred. A maximum of four floors is specified. |
| **Parking**: | 25 staff places<br>25 visitor places |
| **Access**: | Provision must be made for service and supply trucks. As well, provision should be made for a central pickup and drop-off point. |
| **Washrooms**: | One in each room |
| **Cooking Facilities**: | A small kitchenette in each room. This area is to contain a sink, a small refrigerator, a stove, and a microwave oven. |
| **Staffing**: | Staff to resident ratio of 1:20 |
| **Facilities**: | Provision should be made for the following facilities:<br>◆ large lounges for every 50 residents<br>◆ one large dining room with full service and full menu dinners, seating 125 persons at a time<br>◆ library<br>◆ music room<br>◆ crafts room<br>◆ health club room<br>◆ doctor's office<br>◆ nurse's station (one on each floor)<br>◆ kitchen facilities (Access by delivery truck must be considered.)<br>◆ chapel<br>◆ tuck shop<br>◆ administrative offices<br>◆ public washrooms on the main level or off the lobby<br>◆ staff lounge<br>◆ laundry (Access by delivery truck is desired.) |

# Modern Town Planning Primer —Subdivision Plan

Unless topographic difficulties such as ravines, steep hills, swamps, and shorelines exist, the most common street pattern in the older parts of Canadian urban places has been the grid or rectilinear pattern. In Canada, the grid pattern was the popular one used by the British Army engineers and surveyors who planned many of our early settlements.

The grid pattern proved to be the easiest road pattern to survey. Consisting of straight lines and right angles, the grid could be quickly plotted on the landscape, provided a convenient configuration for conventional square or rectangular buildings and lots, and could easily be expanded as the settlement grew.

Unfortunately, this simplicity and ease of implementing the grid has created hundreds of square kilometres of monotonous urban landscapes in Canada. Often the grid has been rigidly applied to sites where the topography is too rugged, resulting in very steep gradients. The gridiron also uses up a tremendous amount of urban land. Up to 30% of the area of an urban place can be taken up by the streets of a grid layout. The many intersections in a grid interfere with the efficient flow of traffic. Although this was not a problem in the nineteenth century when the grid was applied liberally across the landscape and the horse and carriage was the main mode of travel, today, in the era of the automobile, it has resulted in the dreaded traffic "gridlock."

**Figure 34.1 An aerial view of New York city that illustrates the grid pattern.**

Although the grid pattern is well-suited to the downtown areas of large urban places where a formal, well-structured pattern is preferable, there are alternatives available for less congested residential areas.

## The Garden City

Perhaps the first to recognize the problems of unplanned and unregulated urban growth in this century was an Englishman named Ebenezer Howard. In his landmark 1898 work "Garden Cities of Tomorrow," Howard proposed a blending of the best features of both the urban and the rural environments. Although Howard's ideas were often dismissed by critics as overly romantic and unrealistic, the discipline of modern urban planning owes him a great debt. Many of the practices and themes expressed in current planning can be traced back to the thoughts of Ebenezer Howard. Concepts such as green belts, garden cities, land assembly, and neighbourhood and regional planning were introduced by Howard.

 Howard felt that the ideal environment comprised elements from the urban and rural environments and, if these could be combined in one setting, urban living would be vastly improved. Written against the background of the latter years of the Industrial Revolution, the Garden City was presented as an alternative to the tenements and congestion of industrial towns. The countryside, with its fresh air and open spaces, was considered good in contrast to the town with its smoke, soot, poor sanitation, and congestion. The Garden City, as envisioned by Howard, was to be a city in a garden, that is, a city of relatively high density (400 ha in size) surrounded by 2000 ha of countryside. Expenses could be reduced by purchasing less expensive, undeveloped rural land and then increasing its value by installing services, buildings, and people. This, of course, is the forerunner of the practice of land assembly used by developers today. When the population of a Garden City reached a predetermined optimum size (30 000), a new Garden City was to be developed. The landscape would consist of evenly-spaced Garden Cities in a landscape of pastoral countryside. Letchworth Garden City (1903) and Welwyn Garden City (1919) were built to test the concepts introduced by Howard. (See Figures 34.2 and 34.3.) With the framework laid out by Ebenezer Howard, modern urban planning was launched into the twentieth century.

## The Neighbourhood Unit

Clarence Perry working in the United States in the 1920s, realized that most cities grow outwards through accretion and that entirely new planned

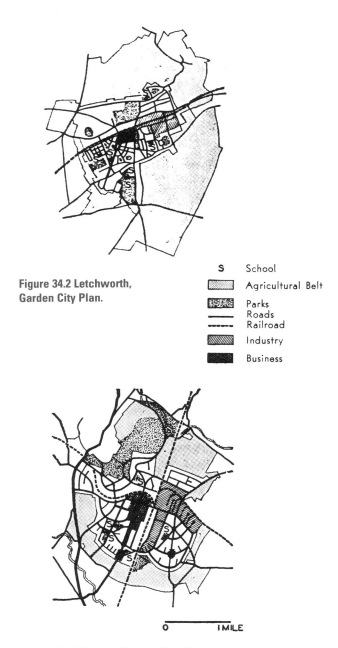

**Figure 34.2 Letchworth, Garden City Plan.**

| | |
|---|---|
| **S** | School |
| | Agricultural Belt |
| | Parks |
| —— | Roads |
| ----- | Railroad |
| | Industry |
| | Business |

0   1 MILE

**Figure 34.3 Welwyn, Garden City Plan.**

communities would be the exception rather than the rule. As a compromise, Perry proposed that smaller neighbourhoods should form the focus of this new growth. These self-contained neighbourhood units were based on four guiding principles:

1. An area equal to 10% of the average 85 ha neighbourhood would be left for open space or parkland.
2. The elementary school would be the focus of the neighbourhood unit and would be within walking distance for the children of the neighbourhood.
3. Heavy traffic producers, such as shopping facilities and apartments, would be located at the outside corners, with single-family detached housing at the centre.

4. Through traffic would be discouraged from passing through the neighbourhood by using extensive dead ends and crescents in the street plan.

In light of the unchecked suburban expansion taking place in the decade following the First World War, Perry's modest suggestions offered some relief from the endless grid being imposed on the landscape. Although quite familiar to us today, Perry's principles of the neighbourhood unit were quite novel when they were introduced.

## The Radburn Plan

Concurrent with the rapid expansion of the suburbs in the twenties was the emergence of the automobile as the prime form of transportation for the average family. The desirability of separating vehicular and pedestrian traffic was reflected in the 1928 design of Radburn, New Jersey. Here Clarence Stein and Henry Wright's objective was to create a "superblock" in which the automobile was confined to the outside of the plan. At the centre of the superblock was a community park. Houses were designed so that they faced the parkland rather than the street. Access to the houses was through small cul-de-sacs on the outside of the plan. (See Figure 34.4.)

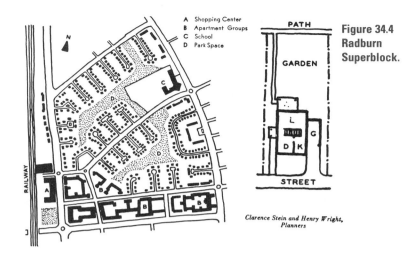

Figure 34.4 Radburn Superblock.

Clarence Stein and Henry Wright, Planners

Although the economic depression of the 1930s meant Radburn was never completed, the "Radburn Plan," as it became known, has been used as a model for many subsequent developments throughout the world. The Radburn Plan was never duplicated in its entirety; however, features of this Classic plan have been incorporated into many other city designs. Stein himself was later to plan the town of Kitimat in the woods of northern British Columbia using the principles demonstrated in the completed portion of Radburn. (See Figure 34.5.)

Figure 34.5 Kitimat, B.C. Plan.

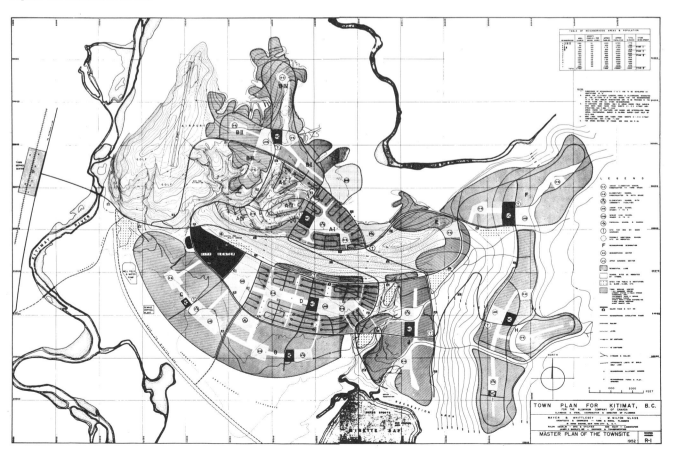

## Broadacre City

The contributions of Perry, Stein, and to some extent, Howard to modern urban planning were based on urban growth of a centralized nature. The neighbourhood and Radburn plans were coping mechanisms, responding to the rapid outward growth of existing cities. In essence, Howard's Garden Cities transferred, although in a much improved form, the city to the countryside. In 1934, the American architect Frank Lloyd Wright proposed a concept that called for a massive decentralization of urban growth. Rather than concentrating people in densely populated cities, Wright suggested that the automobile enabled the population to spread out over a much larger area than previously possible.

Broadacre City, as Wright's concept was called, reflected the long, low prairies style of architecture for which he had received critical acclaim in the early years of the century. Each house was designed as an extension of the landscape. Wright called this *organic architecture*. The ideas proposed in the Broadacre City project can be seen at their best in planned communities where local by-laws prohibit building on less than 1 ha, and at their worst in the suburban sprawl characteristic of most urban places throughout the continent. Wright's intentions certainly were to encourage the former, but the insensitive application of his ideas has more often than not resulted in the latter.

## The Curvilinear and Cluster Patterns

In the Garden City, Radburn, and Neighbourhood plans, the curvilinear street pattern, consisting of curved roads, crescents, and cul-de-sacs, is clearly more sympathetic to the natural topography, following the contours and drainage patterns, if not in fact, at least in spirit. At the same time that it relieved the monotony of the grid, the curvilinear pattern also solved the challenge of traffic flow through the use of a hierarchy of streets, with large arterial roads collecting traffic from collector roads, which in turn, were fed by quiet residential streets. Unless the collector and arterial roads are carefully planned, the pattern that emerges will be logical on paper but will become a labyrinth to those unfamiliar with the area.

In addition to relieving the monotony of the grid, the curvilinear and a variation, the cluster pattern, are often more efficient than the rectilinear street arrangement. (See Figure 34.6.) The cluster is very similar to the ideals proposed in the Radburn Plan. Although individual properties are small, the large communal open space and park-like setting more than compensate for the loss of large lots. Figure 34.7 further illustrates the advantages of the cluster in terms of reducing street length and area and increasing open space and the number of dwellings in a given area.

## Don Mills

It was in Don Mills, Ontario, which in the mid-1950s was the first completely planned new community in Canada, that much of the new thinking in town planning was successfully applied. Incorporating many of the ideas attempted earlier at Radburn, Don Mills became the model of successful suburban planning in Canada. (See Figure 34.8.)

**Figure 34.6 Curvilinear Plan.**

**Figure 34.7 Cluster Plan.**

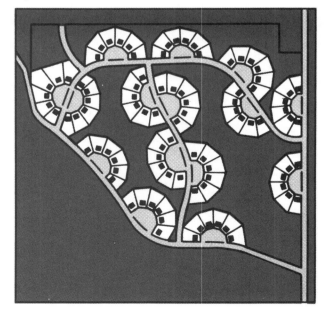

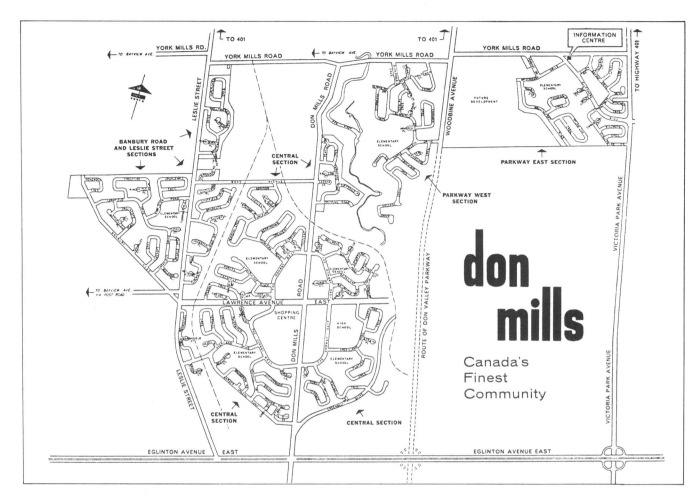

**Figure 34.8 Don Mills Plan.**

The planners of Don Mills pursued a 5-point planning strategy, based largely on the principles proposed in Clarence Perry's Neighbourhood Unit:

1. The main planning focus was to be the neighbourhood, the hub of which was to be the elementary school. Don Mills had four such neighbourhoods designed around a regional shopping mall at the centre.

2. An attempt was made to separate vehicular traffic and pedestrians through the use of the curvilinear street pattern. In Don Mills there are a minimal number of four-way intersections. Most intersections are T-intersections. Extensive walkways further separated vehicles and pedestrians.

3. Green space was an integral part of the plan. The road system was designed in harmony with the landscape. The walkways and open spaces added to the natural feel of Don Mills.

4. Industrial space was to be provided so that residents of the community could work in the community as well. A variety of housing types was required to meet the needs of all employees.

**Figure 34.9 Aerial view of Don Mills, Ontario.**

5. Design standards were to be given careful consideration. All the architectural elements, colours, and materials used were controlled from the outset. One of the more lasting contributions of the Don Mills model was the *Don Mills configuration*, which placed detached houses widthwise to the street. Most suburban housing today reflects this configuration.

**Don Mills configuration**: Macklin Hancock, in designing Don Mills, opted to ignore the standard North York

12 m x 38 m lot in favour of a wider, more shallow 18 m x 30 m lot. On this lot size it was possible to erect a detached house parallel to the street. The increased width of the lot gave more elbow room and the impression of more open space. This arrangement of the house on the lot allowed every house to have a separate driveway. The widthwise placement meant that more windows could be placed in the rather small homes giving the illusion of more space than there really was.

# Applying Planning Models to a Modern Subdivision

## Materials

Site maps (*Blackline Master 34.1*)
Tracing paper or sheets of Mylar
Poster paper or Bristol board
Foamcore

As one of a group of urban planners, you are given the following facts, specifications, and maps to help you plan residential development for a plot of land that has recently become available in a large city. It is expected that you will use the lessons of such models as the Garden City, Radburn, and Don Mills in planning your site. You will be competing with other planners for the lucrative contract to develop the area.

The assignment requires you to complete the following two items:

1. An illustrated, written report of your plan for the area incorporating a title page, an introductory discussion, a plan of a typical housing unit, and a detailed description defending your plan.
2. A model or large-scale map(s) showing the overall plan, as well as selected details of your plan.

Each team of planners will be required to deliver a short explanation of the merits of their plan and will have to be prepared to answer questions from the rest of the class about the details and why their plan should be chosen.

### RESIDENTIAL DEVELOPMENT
#### Specifications

- The site is 20 min by urban transit from the CBD.
- The total area of the site is approximately 11 ha.
- The desired density is 15 housing units per hectare.
- At least 10% of the site must be left as open space.
- No land needs to be reserved for schools, as there is a school nearby.
- Noise from the major artery to the south and east is a concern.
- Soils close to the ravine (within 25 m) are not stable.
- The maximum height allowed for buildings is four storeys.

#### Design Considerations

Your plan for the development should include the following design considerations:

- Plan the street pattern and parking facilities as well as suitable access to the development. (Interior roads should be at least 8 m wide.)
- Based on the natural vegetation map (Figure 34.10), plan the green spaces to be retained in the development. Include provision for benches, playgrounds, pathways, and ornamental gardens. Avoid monotony.
- Plan the location and type of housing (single-detached, condominiums, etc.).
- Make sure that each dwelling has privacy, sunlight, and adequate ventilation. All dwellings must be within two storeys of grade level. In the case of a four-storey building the top two floors would belong to one dwelling unit.
- Plan for at least one parking spot per dwelling and one visitor spot for every five housing units.
- Your plan should fit in with the existing surrounding neighbourhood and not compete with the many turn-of-the-century Victorian semi-detached houses.

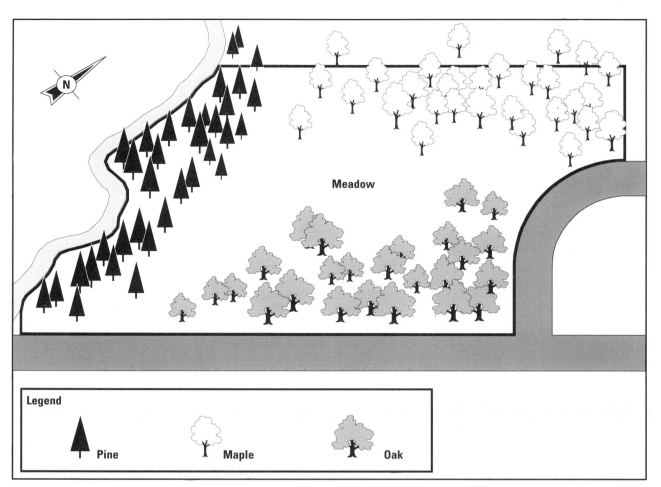

Figure 34.10 A natural vegetation map.

# The Architect's Dream City

There must be days when urban planners wish that they could start all over again in the planning and development of towns and cities. How much easier it would be to develop long range plans based on the knowledge and experience learned from previous endeavours about towns and their growth.

In this last activity you will have an opportunity to begin at the beginning in the development of a new city, a utopian city, unmatched the world over. This is your chance to create a city exactly the way you think a city should be.

For inspiration, you should have at your disposal photographic examples of some of the best architectural styles in the world. Each person working on this activity begins with identical landscape features (BLM 35.1); however, the ultimate "look" and "feel" of the city should be individually yours.

## The Greatest City in the World

### Materials

Base map template for landscape (*Blackline Master 35.1*)
Large sheet of construction paper
Pencil, pen, paint medium of choice

### Preparation

1. Establish criteria and long range goals to support your concept of what a city should be. Consider developing your criteria as an organizer to help you integrate physical, cultural, social, economic, political, and other dimensions of urban life.
2. Investigate some photographic examples of architectural styles and features found in cities of at least four continents. Base your research on some or all of the following categories:

   ◆ religious buildings
   ◆ parks
   ◆ theatres
   ◆ statues
   ◆ fountains
   ◆ museums
   ◆ skyscrapers and other distinctive buildings
   ◆ stadiums
   ◆ towers
   ◆ castles and palaces

Once your photographic research is complete, make template drawings of the features and styles of buildings you have selected to copy and position onto your grid. Create a template only for those categories that are to appear in your city. For example, you need not research stadium photographic references, if stadiums are not structures you are planning to incorporate into the development of your city. Refer back to your long range criteria objectives to clarify your development position.

3. Using 60 squares as a base, establish the amount of space, i.e., number of squares allotted for residential, industrial, commercial, transportation and other special land uses, for your city. Design the breakdown as a graph for easy referencing.
4. Create a grid of 60 squares (4 cm x 4 cm) on a large piece of construction paper. Allow room along the four sides for a broad border. Apply the landscape features shown on the reference base map (BLM 35.1). This grid and base map composition is the foundation for the development of your city.

5. Organize your city, starting with whatever aspects of urban development you consider to be the most essential. Refer to your land use graph to ensure that you are consistent with the aims and objectives you established for land use development. If adjustments are required to the land use graph, make them now before development begins.
6. Name your city.

## Conclusion

1. How do you feel about the way your city developed? Did you accomplish your goals?
2. In small groups, share and compare your city designs. Prepare an organizer to chart the similarities and differences of the city designs in your class.
3. Prepare a two-page paper explaining your rationale for land use as established in a graph earlier in this activity.
4. Is there anything about your city design that you would do differently now that you have viewed other designs? Explain.

## Further Study

1. What have you learned about the challenges of urban development?
2. Evaluate the importance of the many concerned forces at work in an urban centre. What are the urban priorities as you see them? What are the connections between these priorities?
3. If you chose to become politically active in your city, what urban causes would you support? Prepare an oral report to present your platform to others.

# Glossary

**accessibility**: the condition of being easy to reach or get at; the degree to which a place is easy to reach

**active solar gain**: a system of utilizing solar energy that involves an energy input to pump solar heat from rooftop collectors to the interior of the building

**anchor store**: a large store, usually a nationally known department store branch, that serves as an "anchor" or focal point in a shopping mall

**blueprint plan**: a city or building plan, consisting of detail drawings prepared to scale

**break of bulk point**: the location where goods and materials need to be transferred, usually after processing, from one means of transportation to another

**catchment area**: a geographical area served by an institution such as a school

**central business district (CBD)**: that area of an urban centre containing the greatest concentration of offices, shops, and tallest structures; sometimes referred to as "downtown"

**central business height index (CBHI)**: In the Murphy and Vance method of CBD identification the height of buildings housing CBD activities is used in conjunction with central business intensity index to determine whether a city block is classified as CBD.

**central business intensity index (CBII)**: the percentage of the total floor area in a city block devoted to CBD uses; one of the two factors involved in the Murphy and Vance method of CBD identification

**centrifugal**: moving away from the centre; descriptive of a growth pattern moving out from the city centre

**centripetal**: moving toward the centre; descriptive of a growth pattern of attraction toward the city centre

**choropleth map**: a type of map used to show statistical values, with distinctive colours or shading applied to an existing system of area units to indicate the different values

**city**: a large and important town

**cluster pattern**: a residential community pattern in which houses are clustered around communal open spaces along a street, thus reducing street length and increasing housing density

**concentric zone**: a city growth model developed by E. W. Burgess (1925) in which the city is seen as a pattern of five concentric rings growing outward from the city centre

**conurbation**: a large continuous built-up area that is formed when separate towns or cities spread outward and become joined together

**curvilinear pattern**: a street pattern made up of curved roads, crescents, and cul-de-sacs that conform, more or less, to the local topography

**districts**: one of the elements identified by Kevin Lynch as common to most mental maps; areas with homogeneous characteristics, such as neighbourhoods or shopping areas

**Don Mills configuration**: an arrangement of houses in a community that places the homes widthwise to the street, first introduced in the plan for the community of Don Mills, Ontario

**ecological distance**: the distance required to travel between two points when measured in terms of the time and effort involved; the "psychological" distance as opposed to the actual distance

**edges**: one of the five common elements of mental maps identified by Kevin Lynch; refers to the boundaries—real and psychological—found on a mental map, such as neighbourhood boundaries, main streets, and rivers

**exurbia**: a growth area or settlement farther out from the urban centre than the suburbs and spatially distinct from them

**gap point**: the location of a settlement at a point where there is a "gap" or narrow path or passage through or between barriers such as mountains

**garden city**: Ebenezer Howard's plan for an urban community that combined the best features of the city and the countryside, placing the community in a gardenlike setting

**gerontology**: the study of the aging process and the social problems of the elderly

**ghetto**: a city quarter in which members of a minority group live, usually as a result of social, legal or economic pressures

**granny flat**: a type of portable modular cottage, first designed in Australia, for housing elderly parents on the property of their children

**gravity model**: a model for measuring the interaction between urban places mathematically when the population (mass) of each and the distance between them is known

**green belt**: a continuous area of countryside surrounding an urban centre where development is prohibited or strictly controlled

**grid plan**: a city plan in which the streets are laid out as a framework of horizontal and vertical lines perpendicular to one another

**hamlet**: the smallest variety of urban place, usually consisting of a small group of houses together with a few stores and services

**heat sink**: a device for the absorption or dissipation of heat, used in solar homes to store heat collected during the day and to release it at night to warm the building

**heavy industry**: large scale industry involving many employees working in a large plant, such as a steel plant or an automobile factory

**high order good**: a good or service of high value, such as an automobile, which is usually purchased infrequently

**hinterland**: the region lying beyond the boundaries of an urban centre that is served by the urban centre

**human ecology**: a concept developed by the Chicago School to describe the role played by the urban environment in shaping human behaviour

**interurban transportation**: transportation between two urban centres

**intraurban transportation**: transportation within the urban centre

**landmark**: one of Kevin Lynch's five elements common to mental maps; refers to prominent fixtures on the landscape that are used as reference points, such as buildings and monuments

**landscape architecture**: the science and art of landscape design

**land speculation**: the process by which land is set aside or purchased with the intent of seeing its value increase as its use changes or the demand for it increases

**light industry**: industry that involves relatively few employees working in a small plant to produce small-item goods, such as books or computer software

**low order good**: a good or service of relatively low value that is purchased on a regular or frequent basis, such as groceries

**machine space**: space in the urban environment whose primary purpose is for the use of machines, as opposed to human space

**megalopolis**: a huge city formed by the outward growth and merging of several metropolitan cities

**mental map**: the map we carry in our head of the geography of a particular place, neighbourhood, or city; drawings of mental maps give insight into our perception of our urban environment

**morphological distance**: the measurable physical distance between two locations

**morphology**: the form and structure of something; the morphology of an urban place is created by its street patterns, land use patterns, and buildings

**multiple-nuclei model**: a model developed by C. Harris and E. Ullman, that sees the structural pattern of the urban place as a number of decision-making nodes or nuclei

**neighbourhood unit**: a model for new planned communities, proposed by Clarence Perry, involving a self-contained neighbourhood with the elementary school at its centre, with shopping facilities and apartment blocks at the outer corners, a street plan that discourages through traffic, and areas of open space or parkland

**node**: a junction, intersection, or meeting place

**organic architecture**: Frank Lloyd Wright's term for his long, low, prairie architectural style with houses designed as an extension of the landscape

**passive solar gain**: a system of solar energy collection that is integrated into the design of a building and makes use of natural convection currents to warm the building

**paths**: routes to travel from place to place, e.g., roads, sidewalks, and transit routes; one of the five common elements identified by Kevin Lynch in mental maps

**peak value intersection (PVI)**: the intersection in the central business district with the highest land value and usually associated with the highest structures in the city

**people space**: space in the urban landscape destined primarily for people use, as opposed to use for machines or buildings

**point of maximum accessibility (PMA)**: the point in an urban place that is accessible to the greatest number of people, usually the same location as the peak value intersection

**principle of least effort**: the principle that people tend by nature to minimize the inconveniences in distance, cost, and time in their daily operations

**range of a good**: the maximum distance a person is willing to travel to purchase a particular good or service

**rapid transit**: fast means of passenger transportation in urban areas, such as a bus, street car, subway, or train system

**Reilly's Law of Retail Gravitation**: a method of measuring the interaction between two urban places that reflects the consumer attitude that distance discourages and size attracts; a variation of the gravity model

**ring road**: a ring-shaped road, usually designed to carry through traffic around the central business district of an urban centre

**river confluence**: the place where two rivers flow together to form one larger river

**rural-urban fringe**: the area on the outskirts of a city that is neither exclusively rural nor urban, usually an area of land speculation and cash crop farming

**sector pattern**: an urban community model developed by Homer Hoyt in 1939 that divides the urban centre into economic sectors based on real property tax, usually with reference to residential areas of the city

**service centre**: the urban centre to which most people in an area travel to use the services provided there

**site**: the ground on which a structure or a group of structures is, was, or will be located

**situation**: the relationship of a location and its attributes with other reference points or other urban centres

**solar collector**: a device that traps heat from sunlight, commonly used in conjunction with a storage device and a distribution system to provide heating for a building

**spatial interaction**: the interaction between two or more uses of space

**suburb**: a residential area on the outskirts of a city

**superblock**: an urban residential community model, designed by Stein and Wright, for Radburn, New Jersey, in which the houses faced a central community park, with access to the houses through small cul-de-sacs along the outer edge of the block

**threshold of goods or services**: the smallest population required for a business or service to function

**town**: a large village of substantial population and functions, but with lesser status and fewer services than a city

**Trombe Wall**: a solid masonry wall placed behind the glass in a passive solar gain system in a solar house, designed to absorb the incoming solar radiation

**urbanisms**: specialized terminology dealing with elements in the urban environment.

**urban sprawl**: the uncontrolled growth of a city

**village**: a community with fixed boundaries and some local powers of government, larger than a hamlet and smaller than a town

**zoning laws**: regulations aimed at controlling land uses and building in an area

# Acknowledgments

Page  2,   Courtesy Key Largo Film Limitée;
3,   top, Macmillan, London and Basingstoke; bottom, Metropolitan Toronto Library Board;
4,   left, Chemainus Festival of Murals Society; right, Carole Melançon ©, Cartorama enr., Sherbrooke (Quebec);
5,   Royal Ontario Museum;
11,   Novosti Press Agency/B. Kavashkin;
15,   National Archives of Canada/C5648;
18,   The Province of British Columbia;
19,   This map is based on information taken from the National Topographic System Map Sheet Number 92G/6 © 1989.
      Her Majesty the Queen in Right of Canada with permission of Energy, Mines and Resources Canada;
20,   Greater Vancouver Convention Bureau;
21,   top left and centre left, Province of British Columbia;
21,   top right, centre right, and bottom, Carol Waldock;
24,   left, City of Toronto Archives/#1438 "James Collection of Early Canadiana";
24,   right, Aerofilms Ltd., London;
36,   Peter Sander;
38,   Ian Hundey;
40,   Earthcare Enterprise Corporation;
41,   Information & Communication Services Division, Department of the City Clerk, Toronto;
42,   Etobicoke Centennial Park;
46,   Planning Department, City of North York;
49,   Quotation from Barry Garner and Maurice Yates. *The North American City*. New York: Harper and Row, 1976.
52,   The Cadillac Fairview Corporation Limited;
53,   Sherway Gardens, Etobicoke;
57,   Totaro, California Department of Transportation;
59,   Stephanie Berger/NYC Dept. of Transportation;
60,   Peter Mykusz, City of Scarborough;
68,   Foto Flight Surveys Ltd., Calgary;
70,   Noncentral Business District Uses from Murphy and Vance (1954a) Table 2, "Delimiting the CBD," Economic Geography,
      1954. 30:189–222;
73,   Photo courtesy of Montgomery's Inn/City of Etobicoke;
78,   Scarborough Planning Department;
79,   "The Rebel" by Guillermo Mordillo © 1982 OLI-VERLAG NV;
81,   top left, Giancarlo Garofalo, Nino Rico/*Section a*; top right, Alison McKenzie, Helen Vorster/*Section a*; bottom left, Andrea
      Kristof/*Section a*; bottom right, David Stickney/*Section a*;
82,   top, Michael Brisson/*Section a*; bottom, Ken Brooks, David Northcote, Heinz Vogt/*Section a*;
84 and 85,   3 photos courtesy of National Air Photo Library/Energy,
      Mines and Resources Canada;
86,   Collection of the Markham District Historical Museum;
91,   New York Metropolitan Transportation Council;
94,   "Tennis" by Guillermo Mordillo © 1979 OLI-VERLAG NV;
96,   Press Service, Consulate General of France, Toronto;
97,   top, Carol Waldock;
97,   bottom, Japan National Tourist Office;
99,   Scarborough Planning Department;
100,   Photo courtesy of Ian Grainge; Article courtesy of *The Globe and Mail*, Friday, June 22, 1990;
101,   Ed Otten;
105,   Jerome Markson Architects;
107,   New York Metropolitan Transportation Council;
108, and top 109,   VanNostrand Reinhold, reprinted by permission of the Publisher All Rights Reserved;
109,   bottom, District of Kitimat Planning Department;
110,   "Where Not To Build: a guide for open space planning," Technical Bulletin No. 1, United States Department of the Interior,
      Bureau of Land Management, Washington, D.C., April 1968;
111,   top, James Lorimer & Company Ltd.; bottom, Northway Map Technology Limited.

24 HOUR    24 HOUR